THE NEGRO IN OHIO

1802–1870

AMS PRESS

NEW YORK

THE NEGRO IN OHIO

1802—1870

A THESIS

PRESENTED TO THE FACULTY OF THE GRADUATE DEPARTMENT OF

WESTERN RESERVE UNIVERSITY

FOR SECURING THE DEGREE OF DOCTOR OF PHILOSOPHY.

BY

CHARLES THOMAS HICKOK, A.M.

[*Published from the Income of the Francis G. Butler Publication Fund.*]

CLEVELAND, OHIO
1896

Library of Congress Cataloging in Publication Data

Hickok, Charles Thomas, 1869–
  The Negro in Ohio, 1802–1870.

  Thesis—Western Reserve University.
  Reprint of the 1896 ed. published by Williams Publishing &
Electric Co., Cleveland.
  Bibliography: p.
  Includes index.
  1. Negroes—Ohio.   2. Slavery in the United States
—Ohio.   3. Ohio—History—1787–1865.   I. Title.
E185.93.02H6 1975   301.45′19′60730771   79-169487
ISBN 0-404-00064-9

Reprinted from the edition of 1896, Cleveland
First AMS edition published in 1975
Manufactured in the United States of America

AMS PRESS INC.
NEW YORK, N.Y. 10003

To my
father and mother,
whose love and generosity have made the
accomplishment of
this work possible for me.

CONTENTS.

CONTENTS

BIOGRAPHICAL SKETCH.

CHARLES THOMAS HICKOK was born November 8, 1869, at Bloomfield, Ohio. He prepared for college at Shaw Academy, East Cleveland. In 1886 he entered Adelbert College of Western Reserve University, and graduated in 1890, with the degree of Bachelor of Arts. The following year was spent in study at Johns Hopkins University, where he came under the instruction of Professor H. B. Adams and Professor R. T. Ely. In 1891-93, he was instructor in History and Mathematics at Green Spring Academy, then a preparatory school for Adelbert College. In 1892, he received from Adelbert College the degree of Master of Arts. The next year he returned to Western Reserve University and spent two years as a graduate student in the Department of History and Economics. His instructors during this period were Professor E. G. Bourne, Professor H. E. Bourne, Professor M. M. Curtis and Associate Professor S. F. Weston. He served as assistant to the Professor of History, Professor E. G. Bourne. To Professor Bourne he begs to express his deep sense of obligation.

CHAPTER I.

IN December, 1782, a number of the army officers of the Revolution presented a petition to Congress, stating that they were in great financial embarrassment, in consequence of which they and their families were in urgent need. They also complained that mere "shadows had been offered them, while the substance had been gleaned by others." As a reward for their services in defense of their country the petitioners prayed that Congress should devise some mode of redress.* The finances of the country were then very limited, and Congress appeared to be able to do nothing more than to receive the petition and express its sympathy for the petitioners.

A few months later, April 7, 1783, Col. Pickering brought forward a scheme for purchasing from the natives a tract of land lying west of Pennsylvania and north of the Ohio river. He proposed that this territory should be thrown open for settlement to the officers of the Revolutionary army, who should form an association for that purpose ; and further, that a constitution be drawn up for the government of the territory, and suggested that the " total exclusion of slavery from the territory form an essential and irrevocable

---

* Cutler's Life of Manasseh Cutler, 2:154.

part of the Constitution.''*   In this suggestion of Col.
Pickering we have the first glimpse of that principle
of non-slavery which was to characterize the future
Northwest Territory and consecrate that great country north of the Ohio river to liberty and freedom.

Following the propositions of Col. Pickering, a
second petition, signed by 283 officers, was presented
to Congress, praying that land be purchased west
of Pennsylvania and north of the Ohio river, on
which, the petition stated, the officers would make
provision for a settlement.†

The next year, 1784, Virginia empowered her
delegates in Congress to cede all her claims to lands
north of the Ohio.   The deed of cession was executed March 11, 1784.   On that day Congress
appointed a committee to draw up acts for the government of the new territory.   Jefferson was made
chairman of that committee, and on February 21
they were ready to report.‡   The Act reported by
them provided for the establishment of a republican
form of government, which should always be subject
to the government of Congress and the Articles of
Confederation, and should be liable for its full share of
the Federal debt.   And in regard to slavery it stated
that '' after the year 1800 of the Christian era there
shall be neither slavery nor involuntary servitude in
any of said States, otherwise than in punishment
for crimes, whereof the party shall have been duly

---

* Pickering's Life of Timothy Pickering, p. 456; also in the Ap-
pendix to the same, p. 546, where the propositions are printed in
full.

† Cutler's Life of Manasseh Cutler, 2:159.

‡ Barrett's Evolution of the Ordinance of 1787, p. 18.

convicted to have been personally guilty." The
principle set forth by Jefferson plainly does not com-
pare with that of total exclusion, as proposed by Col.
Pickering.

It is a query why Jefferson, who was known to
have held pronounced anti-slavery views, did not
immortalize himself by embracing this opportunity
and embodying in his report the suggestion of Pickering. He may have thought it would be impossible
to secure the consent of Congress for "total exclusion," and so offered his proposition as a compromise. It is not unreasonable, however, to believe
that Jefferson really desired that slavery should exist
in the new territory for a time, for this would encourage his Southern friends to settle there, which
they would not be likely to do, if they could not take
with them their slaves; and this view seems to have
been held by some members of the Convention of
1802, when it was proposed to insert a similar clause
in the Constitution of Ohio. The report presented
by Jefferson was not satisfactory, and it was referred
back to the committee for reconsideration, and when
the second report was made it was moved that the
proviso concerning slavery should be dropped. The
presiding officer, according to the custom of the
times, put the question thus: "Shall the words
stand?" The result, as recorded in Jefferson's own
words, was as follows: "The clause was lost by an
individual vote only. Ten States were present. The
four Eastern States, New York and Pennsylvania,
were for the clause; New Jersey would have been
for it, but there were but two members, and one of
them was sick in his chamber. South Carolina,
Maryland and Virginia voted against it. North

Carolina was tied, as would have been Virginia, had not one of its delegates been sick in bed.'' *

The ordinance divested of its slavery proviso was passed April 23, 1784, and continued in force three years. The friends of freedom were not willing to quietly acquiesce in the decision of Congress. Col. Pickering, who was looking forward to a home for himself west of the Alleghanies, was especially active in keeping alive the opposition against slavery. He wrote earnest letters to Rufus King,† urging him to make another effort to revive the slavery clause of the Ordinance of 1784. He writes to King as follows : "In looking over the act of Congress of the twenty-third of April last, and the present report of an ordinance relative to these lands, I observe there is no provision made for ministers of the Gospel, nor even for schools and academies—the latter might have been brought into view ; though after the admission of slavery, it was right to say nothing of Christianity. To suffer the continuance of slaves until they can be gradually emancipated, in those States where they are already overrun with them, may be pardonable, because unavoidable, without hazarding greater evils —but to introduce them into countries where none now exist can never be forgiven. For God's sake, then, let one more effort be made to prevent so terrible a calamity."‡ Pickering's earnest solicitations were not without results. March 16, 1785, King

---

*Bancroft's Hist. U. S., 4:118 (last ed.), citing letter of Jefferson to Madison, April 25, 1784. The record of vote by names may be found in Barrett's Evolution of Ordinance of 1787, p. 25.

† Delegate from Massachusetts.

‡ Pickering to King, March 8, 1785. Pickering's Pickering, 1:509.

brought forward in Congress the following resolution :

Resolved—"That there shall be neither slavery nor involuntary servitude in any of the States described in the resolution of Congress of the twenty-third day of April, A. D., 1784, otherwise than in punishment of crimes whereof the party shall have been personally guilty ; and that this regulation shall be an article of compact and remain a fundamental principle of the Constitution of the thirteen original States and each of the States described in said resolution of the twenty-third of April, 1784."*

The resolution was referred to a committee of which King was a member. When the action of this committee was reported, it was shorn of its " total exclusion " provision, and allowed slavery to continue till the year 1801, but not after that date. A fugitive slave clause was added, as follows : "Provided always, that upon the escape of any person into any of the States described in the resolution of Congress of the twenty-third day of April, 1784, from whom labor or service is lawfully claimed in any of the original thirteen States, such fugitive might be lawfully reclaimed and carried back to the person claiming his labor or service, this resolve notwithstanding."† But Bancroft says there is no evidence that it was ever called up again in Congress,‡ though Grayson of Virginia, who was a friend of the measure, wrote Madison, " that seven States may be

---

* Barrett, p. 29, citing papers of Old Congress No. 31, p. 327.

† Bancroft Hist. U. S., 6:133, citing papers of Old Congress No. 31, p. 331.

‡ Bancroft's Hist. U. S., 6:134 (last ed.), citing Grayson to Madison, May, 1785.

found liberal enough to adopt it.'' Thus slavery
would have had a legal right to existence in the State
of Ohio till January 1, 1801, had it not been cut short
by the Ordinance of 1787. I have found no evidence
that any ever availed themselves of this right to hold
slaves in Ohio, nor that there was any attempt to
introduce slaves into Ohio till 1799, twelve years
after the Ordinance of 1787 was ratified. Of this
attempt in 1799 and its results I shall speak later.

Notwithstanding Congress failed to act upon either
of the propositions, or petitions, of the Revolutionary
officers, of which I have before spoken, yet help was
to come to them from quite a different source.
March 3, 1786, the Ohio Company was organized.
It was part of the policy of the company to offer
liberal inducements to the army officers to settle in
the new territory. The scheme of the company,
though violently opposed, yet met with considerable
success.*

Emigration to the Western country once begun,
rapidly increased. The need for some form of government was soon apparent both to Congress and to
the company. As early as April, 1786,† Monroe had
secured the appointment of a committee to prepare a

---

* Two pictures went the rounds of the newspapers at this
time, significant of the popular sentiment concerning the "Ohio
Country." They remind one of the "before and after" of the
patent medicine man. The first picture was of a strong, healthy,
hopeful, energetic-looking man bestride a sleek, spirited horse,
saying, "I am going to Ohio." The second picture showed a disappointed, dilapidated, impecunious and malarious man, sitting
on a knock-kneed skeleton of a beast, dejected and mud-stained,
saying, "I have been to Ohio."

† Bancroft says the day on which the motion was made is not
given. That it was probably in April is gained from p. 85, Vol.
xxx., Papers Old Congress.

scheme of temporary government for the Western Territory. This committee progressed rapidly with their work, and on May 9 their report was read a second time. It was at once referred back to the committee for revision and made the order of the next day. It failed to be called up the next day, nor on any succeeding day, till finally the day for adjournment arrived, and nothing had been accomplished. Not till July 4, 1787, did Congress secure a quorum.* On the next day Rev. Manasseh Cutler arrived from New York.† He received a cordial welcome from the members of Congress, and immediately laid before the Committee on Western Lands a petition from the Ohio Company, for a private purchase of land. Mr. Cutler was active in his efforts to interest the members of the committee in the objects of the Ohio Company, and in securing their support for its petition. July 9 the report which was to have been acted upon May 10 was referred to a new committee, Messrs. Carrington, Dane, R. H. Lee, McKean and Smith. This committee drew up and reported to Congress the famous Ordinance of 1787, which was passed by a unanimous vote, July 13. Its principles were embodied in "six articles of compact between the original States, the people, and the States of said territory to remain unalterable, unless by common consent." The first draft of the ordinance as reported by Dane, who appeared to act as clerk of the committee, was silent on the subject of slavery.‡ The renowned anti-slavery

* Bancroft's History of the United States (last edition), 4:285.

† Cutler's Diary, July 5, Life of Cutler, 1:228.

‡ Original draft of the Ordinance in National Intelligencer, August 26, 1847.

clause was added later and formed the sixth section.
The authorship of this clause was for many years
ascribed to Dane, who was supposed to have drawn
up the rest of the ordinance.   But of late years
the subject has been a source of contention.   The
agent of the Ohio Company, Manasseh Cutler, and
Jefferson have both been claimed as its real authors.
In regard to the matter, Dane says in a letter to
Rufus King, " When I drew up the ordinance, which
passed (a few words excepted) as I originally
formed it, I had no idea the States would agree
to the Sixth Article, prohibiting slavery, as only
Massachusetts, of the Eastern States, was present, and I therefore omitted it in the draft—but
finding the House favorably disposed on this subject,
and after we had completed the other parts, I moved
the article, which was agreed to without opposition."*
This at first sight might seem to settle the question of
authorship ; the problem, however, still remains—was
Dane the author of the article which he as spokes-
man of the committee "moved," or was it the joint
product of the whole committee, or was it derived
from a source entirely outside of the committee? Daniel Webster at one time pronounced an encomium on
the Ordinance of 1787 and ascribed to Dane the honor
of the sole authorship. †   The accuracy of his statement was promptly challenged by Mr. Benton of
Missouri.   " Before I proceed," said Mr. Benton,
" to the main subject of this reply, I must be permitted to clear away some ornamental work and
remove some rubbish which the Senator from Massachusetts [Mr. Webster] has placed in the way,

*Life of Cutler, 1:372.
† Webster's Works, 3:264.

either to decorate his own march or to embarrass
mine. He has brought before us a certain Nathan
Dane of Beverly, Mass., loaded him with such an
exuberance of blushing honors as no modern name
has been known to merit or to claim. So much
glory was caused by a single act, that act, the supposed authorship of the Ordinance of 1787, and
especially the clause in it which prohibited slavery
and involuntary servitude; so much encomium and
such grateful consequences it seems a pity to spoil,
but spoiled they must be, for Mr. Dane was no more
the author of that ordinance, Sir, than you or I,
who about that time were muling and puking in our
nurses' arms. That ordinance, and especially the
non-slavery clause, was not the work of Nathan
Dane of Massachusetts, but of Thomas Jefferson of
Virginia."* Inasmuch as Jefferson was absent from
the country in 1787, as United States Minister to
France, it is difficult to make for him a satisfactory
case. The eloquent outburst of Benton must be
ascribed to extreme partisan prejudice, rather than
to any definite historical knowledge of the subject.
The claims for Mr. Cutler merit more careful consideration; his biographers certainly make out a
strong case for him and it would seem highly probable that at least he aided in the authorship by way
of suggestion to Mr. Dane and the other members
of the committee. Mr. Poole, in the article referred
to, cites a letter, January 30, 1847, from Dr. Joseph
Torrey, a son-in-law of Mr. Cutler, to Judge
Ephraim Cutler of Ohio. Dr. Torrey writes " that
he had seen a large pile of Ohio documents, among

---

*Quoted by W. F. Poole in article "Dr. Cutler and Ordinance
of 1787," North American Review, 122:235.

these the Ordinance of 1787, on a printed sheet, and
on its margin was written that Mr. Dane requested
Mr. Cutler to suggest such provision as he deemed
advisable, and at Mr. Cutler's instance was inserted
what relates to religion, education and slavery."*
It would appear from the above that Dane, being on
friendly terms with Cutler, asked his advice respecting this matter, which he knew would especially
interest him, a resident in the new territory.   Surely
this much can be allowed, that Dane, as clerk of the
committee, drew up the ordinance, and finding the
members of the committee favorably disposed, added
with their consent the sixth section, which had been
suggested to him. If the suggestion came from
Cutler, then the chief honor should belong to him.
But it is perfectly obvious that the actual composition of the article was not entirely original with
either Dane or Cutler, for the phraseology is similar
to that used by Jefferson in his rejected slavery
proviso, in the Ordinance of 1784, and also to King's
amended resolution of April 26, 1784.†

Rejected proviso of Jef-
ferson in Ordinance of
1784.
"After the year 1800 of
Christian era *there shall be
neither slavery nor involuntary servitude in any of
said States, otherwise than
in punishment of crimes*

Sixth Article of Ordi-
nance of 1786.
"There shall be neither
slavery nor involuntary

---

* Cutler's Life of Manasseh Cutler, 2:343, quoted by Poole in
his article in North American Review, 122:261.

† I subjoin here the three for comparison. The words italicized
in Jefferson's proviso and in King's resolution are common to
the Sixth Article.

*whereof the party shall
have been duly convicted.*"
Amended resolution of
King, April 26, 1784.

"Resolved, that after the
year 1800 of the Christian
era there *shall be neither
slavery nor involuntary
servitude* in any of the
States described in the resolve of Congress of the
twenty-third day of April,
1784, *otherwise than in
punishment of crimes
whereof the party shall
have been personally guilty;*
and that this regulation
shall be an article of compact, and remain a funda-
mental principle of the
Constitution between the
thirteen original States and
each of the States described
in the said resolve of Congress of the twenty-third
day of April, 1784, any
implication or construction
of the said resolve, to the
contrary notwithstanding.
Provided always upon the
escape of any person into
any of the States described
in said resolve of Congress
of the twenty-third day of
April, 1784, *from whom
labor or service is lawfully
claimed in any one of the
thirteen original States,
such fugitive may be law-
fully reclaimed* and carried
back *to the person claiming
his labor or service as aforesaid*, this resolve notwith
standing."

servitude in the said territory, otherwise than in
punishment of crimes
whereof the party shall
have been duly convicted;
provided always, that any
person escaping into the
same, from whom labor or
service is lawfully claimed
in any one of the original
states, such fugitive may
be lawfully reclaimed and
conveyed to the person
claiming his or her labor
or service as aforesaid."

On July 13, 1787, the ordinance received the assent
of every one of the eighteen members present, excepting Abraham Yates, the younger, of New York,
who, says Bancroft, "insisted on leaving to all
future ages a record of his want of good judgment,
right feeling and common sense."* It seems very
remarkable that the ordinance should have received
such a unanimous approval, where five of the eight
States present were Southern, and naturally would
be opposed to the anti-slavery proviso.† Much
speculation has been indulged in by historical writers
concerning the motives which determined the vote
of the Southern members. Probably we shall never
be able to obtain an explanation which will be complete and final. Among the motives which
actuated their vote, we may reasonably believe,
was the fact that anti-slavery feeling at that
time was not monopolized by the North.
William Grayson of Virginia had voted in favor of
King's resolution of March 16, 1785, and earnestly
supported the Ordinance of 1787. Slavery had not
then become the "peculiar institution" of the South,
to be zealously fostered and defended from every
Northern attack. Thomas H. Benton maintains that
Southern States voted against Jefferson's proposed
slavery proviso in the Ordinance of 1784, simply
because there was no provision in it for the return of
fugitive slaves. But when this was provided for, as
it was in the new Ordinance of 1787, the Southern States willingly voted for it.‡ Benton implies

*Bancroft's Hist. U. S., 4,290.
†The States present were Georgia, South Carolina, North Carolina, Virginia, Delaware, New York, Massachusetts, Pennsylvania and Maryland, and three States of New England were absent.
‡Benton's Thirty Years in the United States Senate, 1:133, 135.

that the South had always desired to curtail slavery
and restrict it to the Southern States, provided their
local property could be protected from escape.   No
doubt there is considerable truth in this, but if it was
the prevailing sentiment, Jefferson, who was one of
the Southern members, must have known it in 1784,
when he proposed the resolution allowing slavery
till 1800.   He professed to be greatly disappointed
at the rejection of his slavery proviso, yet he could
easily have added a fugitive slave clause, if that
would have secured the passage of his proviso.   I
cannot think that the disposition to limit the extension of slavery, provided that the local property
could be protected, was sufficiently general in the
South at that time to justify us in attributing to it
alone the reason for the Southern vote.   Some light
is thrown on this perplexing question by a letter
written by Grayson to Monroe, August 8, who,
as a member of the committee confirming the ordinance, was in a position to know why the Southern
members voted as they did.   He writes: "The
clause respecting slavery was agreed to by the Southern members for the purpose of preventing tobacco
and indigo from being raised on the northwest side
of the Ohio river, as well as for several political
reasons."*   Here are reasons assigned by one of the
members themselves of quite a different character
from those given above by Benton.   Indigo and
tobacco were then two of the most profitable agricul-
tural products.   The South thought slave labor to be
indispensable to their cultivation.   If slavery should
be excluded from the territory north of the Ohio, it

_____

*Cited by Dunn in his most valuable History of Indiana,
p 212.

would rapidly fill up with a population from the
Eastern States, which would open a new market for
Southern products, the raising of which could be
monopolized by the South. We now find the motives entirely shorn of their philanthropic character
with which Benton had surrounded them. They
appear, according to Grayson's own confession, to
be those of self-interest. So much can be allowed,
but I do not think we should stop here. It does not
seem probable that the reason given by Mr. Grayson
would, unprompted, have occurred to all the members simultaneously. Mr. Dane tells us that he had
no idea that the members would assent to an anti-
slavery clause, and so left it out of his first draft, but
" finding the House favorably disposed on the subject, I moved it." I ask, does it not look as if some
" lobby work " had been done among the members?
The benefits which might accrue to the South by the
exclusion of slavery from the new territory were
certainly, as yet, in the dim future. Judging by the
rate of emigration to the West at this time, the South
had no cause to fear Western competition in the cultivation of tobacco and indigo. These products
could be more profitably raised on large plantations
where the soil could be kept enriched or allowed to
rest by the rotation of crops, or where there was opportunity for the removal to new and unworked
fields. As a fact, tobacco was raised north of the
Ohio equal in quality to any raised in the South.
Here then was a vast and practically unoccupied
country, whose virgin soil would yield for years an
abundant harvest, and the Southern planter could
reasonably have anticipated immediate returns by
encouraging emigration to such a country, and yet

he voted to deny himself present advantages for future ones, which he hoped would be greater and more lasting. That this is correct policy we would not deny, but men generally prefer the "one bird in the hand to two in the bush." Southern statesmen were not usually so far-sighted; if they had been they would have shown more of a disposition to have done away with slavery altogether, for men were not lacking in the South who believed the institution of slavery a curse, and that its removal would ultimately prove an inestimable benefit to them. I am impressed that some influence was brought to bear on the Southern members of the committee, which convinced them that their own interest would be better secured by the exclusion of slavery from the new territory. From what source did this influence come? Certainly not from Mr. Dane, for he thought his brethren from the South would not listen to any restriction or exclusion of slavery. In my opinion, Mr. Grayson of Virginia and Dr. Cutler of the Ohio Company were the two men who were largely influential in securing the unanimous vote of the Southern members for the Ordinance of 1787. Grayson, as we have seen, had already given evidence of his anti-slavery feelings. He had heartily supported the ordinance, and being a Southerner himself, would naturally on that account have been able to exercise a considerable influence among his brother members. The biographers of Dr. Cutler make out a very plausible claim for him. They attribute the result of the vote almost entirely to his own personal influence. This claim is no doubt too sweeping, but the evidence is reasonable that Dr. Cutler had no small part in determining the vote of July 13, 1787.

He came to New York with more than forty letters of introduction to prominent men, by whom he was cordially received.   In his journal he writes that he found the Southerners masters of the situation, and that he gave special attention to Carrington, Lee, Grayson and other "members from the South-ward." No one could have had more personal interest in the passage of the ordinance than he, and if it may be allowed that he suggested the Sixth Article and urged its acceptance by the committee, it would be most natural for him to work for its final approval by Congress.

I am led therefore to assign three reasons for the passage of the ordinance :

First—Slavery was regarded at this time by the South as a necessary and hereditary evil ; the eco-nomic or political reasons for defending and extending it which arose six years later, after the invention of the cotton gin, did not then exist.

Second—The economic advantages which the South believed would be derived from a monopoly of tobacco and indigo cultivation, and further, the settlement of the Northwest would open up new markets for Southern staples.

Third—The personal influence which Dr. Cutler, aided by Mr. Grayson of Virginia, exerted upon the committee and other members.

There is another principle of the ordinance which must always be considered in connection with the Sixth Article.   Had it not declared that the articles shall be considered articles of compact* the prohibi-

---

* "Between the original States and the people and the States of the new territory, to remain unalterable, unless by common consent.'

tion would probably have become a dead letter,
and Indiana and possibly Ohio would have been
slave States. As far as I can learn, Ohio made no
direct attempt to secure a suspension of the sixth
clause, but Indiana repeatedly petitioned Congress
for a suspension of the clause.

As early as 1802 a convention of delegates from
different parts of Indiana, presided over by Governor
Harrison, voted to send a memorial to Congress,
praying for a repeal, or at least a suspension of the
slavery prohibition. The memorial stated that the
citizens of Indiana found themselves greatly ham-
pered in the competition with their brethren south
of the Ohio river, since cheap labor was absolutely
necessary to insure the growth and prosperity of a
new State. The memorial was referred to a committee, of which John Randolph of Virginia was
chairman. They reported to the effect that "the
rapid growth of Ohio did not justify the necessity for
slave labor to promote the growth and settlement
of the Northwest territory, and that they could not
but deem it highly inexpedient and dangerous to
impair a provision wisely calculated to promote the
happiness and prosperity of the Northwest territory,
and that Indiana would at no distant day find ample
remuneration for the temporary privation of slave and
consequent emigration." *

The next year, Indiana made another effort to
secure a suspension of the obnoxious article, but
without success. Again in 1804 she sent a similar
petition to Congress. The House Committee, to
which the petition was referred, reported in favor of

---

* American State Papers : Public Lands, 1:160.

granting its prayer; but before taking action the
House moved its commitment to a select committee.
The petition was presented March 17, 1804, and in
just two years, lacking three days, the select committee returned its report.* In the meantime
another petition had been sent by the inhabitants
of Indiana, and also one accompanied by resolutions
from the Legislative Council of the territory, all
praying that the Sixth Article might be suspended.

The committee, no doubt influenced by this evidence of determination, reported that in its opinion it
would be to the interest of Indiana and of the whole
country to grant the prayers of the petitioners. It
was not a question of slavery or freedom, for slavery
already existed; and if it was an evil, the evil would
not be increased by its entrance into Indiana. On
the contrary, the condition of the slaves would be
greatly ameliorated, for experience has shown that
the more they are separated, the more care and
attention they receive from their masters. Beside,
the dangers arising from the increase of negroes in
the South would be lessened, while there was little
to fear that their numbers in the territory of Indiana
would ever be great enough to threaten its safety.
" Therefore the committee would recommend that
the Sixth Article of the Ordinance of 1787, which
prohibits slavery in the territory of Indiana, be
suspended for ten years." This same committee
reported adversely to a petition from the inhabitants
of Indiana to be annexed to the State of Ohio.† I
have not been able to find that any action was ever
taken on the report of the committee. Had Congress

---

* March 14, 1806.

† American State Papers: Miscellaneous, 1:451.

granted the petition and united Indiana to Ohio, who
can say what changes would have followed in the
history of that State. If only the original petition for
suspension had been acceded to, momentous consequences must have been the result. Had Ohio
been bordered on two sides by slave States, with the
inhabitants of the southern part strongly bound to the
South by social and business relations, a strong pressure would have been brought to bear to secure for
Ohio, too, a suspension of slavery prohibition. The
sacredness of the ordinance once violated, it would
have been comparatively easy for each and all of the
other States, formed out of the Northwest territory,
to have obtained a like suspension ; and all that
section so uniquely consecrated to freedom would
have been turned over to slavery. The Indiana
Legislature, however, was by no means willing
to have all this effort go by default, and was
determined to keep the matter before the members of Congress. They, therefore, the next
year, 1807, sent another petition to Congress from
the Legislature, reiterating the advantages which
they had previously claimed would result to the
slave and to the State by the suspension of the Sixth
Article. But by this time no little opposition had
been aroused among the citizens of the State against
these repeated attempts to introduce slavery into their
midst. A mass meeting was held at Springfield, Clark
county, October 10, 1807,* at which time counter
resolutions were passed and a petition drawn up and
forwarded to Congress, declaring that the Territorial
Legislature had misrepresented the sentiment of the
people ; that they were by no means unanimously in

---

* Dunn's Indiana, p. 358.

favor of suspension, and praying Congress not to
grant the petition of the Legislature. This petition
from the people and the petition from the Legislature were referred by the Senate to the appropriate
committee. November 13, 1807, it brought in the
following brief, conclusive report:

Resolved—" That it is not expedient at this time
to suspend the Sixth Article of the compact for the
good of the territories of the United States northwest
of the Ohio river.''*

The use of the word '' compact '' in this report,
instead of ordinance, as was customary, throws light
on the real opinion of the committee respecting the
binding force of the ordinance ; it also tended to
show that any attempt to break the '' compact ''
would always prove futile. I have been unable to
find that any further effort was made to secure the
suspension of the slavery clause, and the question
was thus definitely and finally settled, as far as any
further efforts were made by the State of Indiana.

The expediency of introducing slavery for a short
period, as reviewed in the history of Indiana, is intimately connected with the history of the negro in
Ohio, inasmuch as it reveals the opinion of a considerable portion of the people of the whole Northwest Territory on that subject. The early settlers of
Ohio were largely from the Eastern States, where
climate and industrial conditions rendered slavery
unprofitable, and it was therefore rapidly dying out ;
and by their surroundings and education they were
unaccustomed to slave labor, and had no disposition
to abrogate the provisions of the Ordinance of 1787.

---

*American State Papers; Miscellaneous, 1:484.

On the contrary, Indiana was largely peopled by emigration south of the Ohio river, and it was by no means unnatural that they should wish to introduce an institution with which they were familiar in their old home. They no doubt honestly thought that emigration would be stimulated, and the material growth of the territory would be advanced by the introduction of slavery for a limited time. Ill-judged as their convictions might have been, they were, without question, sincerely held ; but had these convictions become the established laws of the State, the result on the future of Ohio would have been overwhelming.

The New England settlers of Ohio were pioneers, not only in the work of opening a new and almost unknown country and laying foundations for a future State, but they were among the few people who ever blazed a path through the wilderness, cleared the forests and planted the fields without the help of slave labor or ever once attempting to introduce it. From the first, Ohio was an inviting country for emigration, and it is not surprising that as early as 1799, during the first session of the Territorial Legislature, certain Virginia officers of the Revolution sent up a memorial, praying for the privilege of occupying the military bounty lands lying between the Scioto and the Little Miami rivers with their slaves. Thus the question of introducing slavery confronted the Legislature of Ohio in its first session, and it must be squarely met. According to the Sixth Article of the Ordinance of 1787, the Legislature could not do otherwise than refuse the petition—and it did.

Mr. Jacob Burnett, who was a member of the Legislature, gives us a very clear idea of the senti-

ment of its members and the prevailing opinion of
the people of the territory on the subject. He says,
"Their only course was to reject the petition,
although it was apparent that if the application of the
memorialists could have been granted, it would have
brought into the territory a great accession of wealth,
strength and intelligence, yet the public feeling on
the subject of admitting slaves was such that the
request would have been denied by a unanimous vote
of the Legislature, had they possessed the power of
granting it. They were not only opposed to slavery
on the ground of its being a moral evil, in violation
of personal rights, but were of the opinion that whatever might be its immediate advantages, it would
ultimately retard the settlement and check the prosperity of the territory, by making labor less respectable and creating feelings and habits unfriendly to
the simplicity and industry they desired to encourage
and perpetuate."*

When we consider that slavery legally was nearly
co-extensive with the United States, we can better
appreciate that the position taken by the infant territory of Ohio was greatly in advance of that held by
most of her older sister States. In 1801 the Legislature had again an opportunity to declare itself
respecting slavery. Two petitions were presented,
praying that a clear declaration be made of the true
meaning of the Sixth Article of the Ordinance of
1787, and by an enactment authorize the courts to
compel the performance of the contracts for service
entered into for a compensation. It seemed evident
that the petitioners wanted to covertly secure the
sanction of the Legislature for some form of slavery,

---

* Burnett, Notes on Northwest Territory, p. 306.

either by indenture or contract. Again the "Honorable Body" firmly planted itself on the principle of "total exclusion" and laid the petition on the table, and Mr. Burnett says, with the understanding that it should not be taken up again. Several members of the State Convention, which framed the Constitution the following year, were members of this territorial legislature, and their influence seems apparent in the second article of the eighth section, relative to the prohibition of indenture of colored persons.* Thanks to the wise and beneficent principles of the Ordinance of 1787, Ohio closed her territorial history with an unbroken record of determined opposition against every effort to introduce slavery under any form, or to any extent within her borders.

I cannot close this chapter on the Ordinance of 1787 in any way better than by quoting that splendid encomium which was pronounced upon it by Daniel Webster in his first speech on the "Foot Resolutions." "It fixed forever the character of the population of that vast region northwest of the Ohio river, by excluding from them involuntary servitude. It impressed upon the soil itself, while it was yet a wilderness, an incapacity to sustain other than freedom. It laid the interdict against personal servitude in an original compact, not only deeper than all local laws, but deeper than all local institutions.

"We are accustomed, Sir, to praise the law-givers of antiquity; we help to perpetuate the fame of Solon and Lycurgus, but I doubt whether any single law by any law-giver, ancient or modern, has produced effects of more distinct, marked and lasting character than the Ordinance of 1787."†

* Burnett's Notes, p. 333.
† Delivered in U. S. Senate, January 20, 1830. Webster's Works, 3:263.

CHAPTER II.

THE Ordinance of 1787 passed, it remained for
Congress to inaugurate the government established by that document. October 5 of the same
year General Arthur St. Clair was appointed Governor of the new Territory. Early in July, 1788,
he was cordially welcomed by the inhabitants of
the territory, and entered upon his work. One of
his duties was the appointment of three judges, who
should preside over the territorial court.

September 2 the Judiciary was formally inaugu-
rated.* By the provisions of the ordinance the
governor and judges should form a temporary legislative body. They were not empowered to enact
new laws, but to adopt and publish such laws, then
existing in the original States, as were best adapted
to the needs of the district. When the territory
attained a population of 5,000 this temporary legislative council was to be superseded by a general
assembly, elected by all the free male inhabitants.
In 1798 it was found that the territory possessed the
requisite population. A territorial legislature was
accordingly elected, and held its first session in Cincinnati, September 24, 1799. During this session the

---

*Hinsdale, Old Northwest, p. 287.

32

Virginia officers presented the memorial referred to in the previous chapter. I have been unable to learn that there was any discussion in the assembly concerning slavery or free negroes for the next two years. In 1801 was presented the petition praying for legislation upon the true meaning of the ordinance. Of the fate of that petition we have already spoken. These two occasions, *i. e.*, 1799 and 1801, were the only times when the question of slavery or the status of the free negro received any formal attention from the Ohio Territorial Legislature. In 1802 a census of the population was taken, and it was found that the population had increased to 45,028.* Accordingly a petition was sent to Congress asking for admission as a State. Notwithstanding the opposition of many to the formation of a State Government at that time, Congress promptly passed the necessary legislation. A convention was called to draft a State Constitution. This convention met in Chillicothe, November 1, 1802, and proceeded at once to the business before them, but our knowledge of the real work accomplished by this convention is extremely limited. The minutes which were kept were very brief and conspicuously incomplete. Judge Burnett, in his "Notes on the Northwest Territory," conveys the impression that the status of the negro was never an actual issue in the convention. But imperfect as the minutes were, enough can be gathered to make it evident that the prospective status of the negro elicited some lively discussions.

The report of the committee on electoral qualifications granted suffrage only to the "white male in-

---

*Hinsdale, Old Northwest, p. 318.

habitants.''* A motion was immediately offered
to strike out the word ''white.'' The motion was
lost by only five votes.†

The result shows that there was no small element
in the convention favorable to the negro, and desirous of encouraging his emigration to the new State,
and this conclusion is confirmed by a second motion
being made immediately upon the defeat of the first.
This motion proposed to make an exception in favor
of the negroes already resident in the State, provided
that within a specified time they made a record of
their citizenship.‡ This motion was carried, the
vote being almost the reverse of that of the preceding motion.§ The friends of the black man, thus
encouraged, hoping to extend the same privilege to
the descendants of resident negroes, offered a third
motion to this effect: '' Provided that the male
descendants of such male negroes and mulattoes as
shall make record shall be entitled to the same
privilege.'' The motion was defeated by a single
vote.‖ Eventually the proviso was rescinded. Upon

*Constitution of 1802, Art. iv., Sec. 1. In all elections all
white male inhabitants . . . shall enjoy the right of an
elector . . .

†The vote stood 14 to 19 against. The minutes of the convention are exceedingly rare; only a few copies are known to be in
existence. The editors of the Historical Magazine have very
appropriately reprinted them in their issue of July, 1869. Pages
of the minutes referred to in the text are of the Historical
Magazine.

‡ The following proviso was to be attached to the first section,
Art. iv.: ''Providing that all male negroes or mulattoes now residing in the Territory shall be entitled to the right of suffrage if
they shall within —— months make a record of their citizenship.''
Minutes, p. 21.

§ The vote stood 19 to 15 against.

‖ Vote stood 16 for, 17 against. Minutes, p. 21.

the second reading it was moved to strike it out; the vote resulted in a tie, but by vote of the President* it was decided in the affirmative. The negro in Ohio was thus excluded from all participation in the electoral privilege of a citizen. Though denied the privileges, he had the consolation that he escaped the duties of citizenship. The convention was not, however, so ungenerously disposed as to impose "taxation without representation," for we find that a motion was made to add a seventh section to the article, comprehending general provisions and regulations, declaring that negroes should never be subject to military duty or be required to pay a poll tax. At the same time, as an offset to this generous concession, it declared him ineligible to any office, civil or military, and prohibited him from giving evidence in any court against a white person. The proposed article closed with the rather ironical statement that all negroes resident in the State, or who should become residents, were to be entitled to all the privileges of citizens which were not excepted by the Constitution.† The negro was permitted to get all the consolation out of this that was possible. The clause was carried,‡ but in the second reading a

---

* Minutes, p. 24.

† Proposed Sec. 7: "No negro or mulatto shall ever be eligible to any office, civil or military, or give their oath in any court of justice against a white person, or be subject to military duty, or pay a poll tax in this State. Provided always, and it is fully understood and declared that all negroes or mulattoes now in, or who may ever reside in this State, shall be entitled to all the privileges of the citizens of this State not excepted by the Constitution. Minutes, p. 22.

‡ Vote stood 19 for, 16 against; motion to strike out, vote stood 17 for, 16 against.

motion was made to strike it out, and to the honor
of Ohio the motion was sustained.

Later an effort was made to revive the above section, but was fortunately decided in the negative.*

A moment's reflection upon the votes taken on the
respective propositions regarding the negro shows
that there was great diversity of opinion, but no
fixedness of judgment, among the members of the convention ; there was continual shifting from one side
to the other.   The sentiment of the country regarding slavery was in a transitional stage.   The invention of the cotton gin a few years before had made
slave labor immensely more profitable.   The South
was struggling to make over its old creed to meet the
new conditions, while the North, startled and perhaps a little jealous of the growing prosperity of the
South, was beginning to see the wrong of a system
which the South was soon to regard with increasing
favor, and to look upon as an economic blessing.
The discussions regarding the status of the negro
inhabitants were exciting such warmth of feeling in
the convention that fears were entertained that the
object for which they were assembled would be
wholly defeated. " The apprehension of such a disas-
trous result," says Burnett, " induced the members to
abandon all the propositions which had been made,
and to proceed to form a constitution having no
direct reference to that matter, but embracing only
the free white population, who alone were represented
in the body." †

A convention convened to draw up a constitution

---

* The provision regarding negro testimony in court was, a
few years later, embodied in the statute laws of the State. See
Act of Ohio Legislature, January 25, 1802.

† Burnett's Notes, p. 355.

for a State, which was to be carved out of the North-west Territory, naturally would not adjourn without in some way settling the question of slavery in the new State. There were those in the convention and in the country who maintained that the provisions of the Ordinance of 1787 were binding on the district only as a territory, and consequently that Ohio, as a State, was free to determine for herself whether she should admit or exclude slavery. There were others who thought that the growth of the State would be greatly quickened by allowing Southern planters to immigrate with their slaves, hence they were desirous to sanction slavery for a term of years. The question was finally brought to an issue by John W. Brown, who submitted to the Committee on Forma-tion of Bill of Rights, of which he was chairman, a proposition which defined the subject in effect thus: That no person should be held in slavery, if a male, after he was thirty-five years of age, and if a female, after she was twenty-five years of age. It is obvious that Mr. Brown believed, or pretended to believe, that the territory, upon erection into a State, was immediately freed from the obligations and prohi-bitions of the Ordinance of 1787. His section simply purports to regulate the operations of an institution already legally recognized. Judge Cutler, son of Manasseh Cutler, who was also a member of this committee, observed to his fellow members that his constituents wanted this subject clearly under-stood, and consequently he moved to lay the section on the table till the next meeting; in the meantime, that each member should prepare a section which should fully express his views upon the subject. The next morning when the committee met, Judge

Cutler was called upon for what he had prepared.
What followed, I give in his own words: "I then
read to them the section as it now stands in the Constitution. Mr. Brown observed that what he had
introduced was thought by the greatest men in the
nation to be, if embodied in the Constitution, a great
step toward the emancipation of slavery, and was in
his opinion greatly to be preferred to what I had
offered."*

The section as prepared by Judge Cutler was
finally adopted by the committee by a vote of five to
four. When it came before the convention several
attempts were made to weaken or obscure the true
sense of the section, and the debate became so spirited and so much opposition was aroused, that Judge
Cutler, fearing the section would be lost, and hoping
to save something, moved to strike out the more
obnoxious portions, but one delegate changed his
vote when the call was made, and the section was
finally passed in its original form, by only one vote.
Thus twice, once in the committee and again in the
convention, one vote saved Ohio from the disgrace
and calamity of being burdened by some form of
negro slavery. To Dr. Manasseh Cutler is due in
part at least the honor and gratitude of proposing
and urging the adoption of the Sixth Article of the
Ordinance of 1787, which consecrated the Northwest
territory to freedom. To his son, Ephraim Cutler,
was reserved the glory of framing and aiding in the
insertion of a similar article in the Constitution of
the State of Ohio.† Not only was slavery forever

*Life of Ephraim Cutler, p. 75.
† Constitution, Art. viii., Sec. 2: "There shall be neither slavery nor involuntary servitude in the State, otherwise than for

prohibited, but care was taken that neither by indenture nor any kind of apprenticeship should any kind of slavery ever gain a foothold within the borders of the State of Ohio.

To any one reading the Constitution of 1802, it is clear that the framers intended the negro to occupy the same relation to the Government that the Indian or unnaturalized foreigner did. They were permitted to live in the State and the protection of the laws was offered them, but in the government of the State they had no part. Civic duties were not to be demanded of them nor any of the distinctive privileges of a citizen to be allowed them. Such was the status of the negro in Ohio when the State was admitted to the Union, November 29, 1802. The number of negroes in the State at the time was very small.* There was not more than

---

punishment of crimes whereof the party shall have been duly convicted. Nor shall any male person arrived at the age of 21 years, or female person arrived at the age of 18 years, be held to serve any person as servant under pretense of indenture or otherwise, unless such person shall enter into such indenture while in a state of freedom, and on condition of a *bona-fide* consideration received for their service, except as before excepted. Nor shall any indenture of any negro or mulatto, hereafter made or executed out of the State, or made in the State, where term of service exceeds one year, be of the least validity, except those given in cases of apprenticeship."

* According to the U. S. census, the following is the number of white and colored inhabitants in Ohio from 1800 to 1870:

YEARS.	WHITE.	COLORED.
1800	45,028	337
1810	227,861	1,890
1820	576,572	4,723
1830	928,093	9,586
†1840	1,502,125	17,342
1850	1,955,050	25,279
1860	2,302,808	36,673
1870	2,601,946	63,213

one black man to every 110 white persons. During the next ten years the colored population rapidly increased, but was confined almost wholly to the counties bordering on the Ohio river. In the northern part of the State, until after the Civil War, the negro was quite a novelty in the country districts ; in the cities they were not numerous.*

As early as 1804, during the second session of the Legislature, attention was called to the increasing immigration of colored people into the State. This ingress of free negroes 'was looked upon by many as a great calamity. From the beginning the Southern counties had received a large proportion of their settlers from Kentucky and Virginia, and by them the free blacks were always regarded as despicable and entitled neither to the respect nor charity of the whites. There was also another contingent who, while not Southern themselves, were so bound to them by social and business relations that they could always be relied upon by the South for sympathy and support. The influence of these two classes was great enough to secure in this Legislature a bill which should tend to restrict negro immigration, in reality, a fugitive slave bill. This feature, no doubt, was in response to complaints from Kentucky and Virginia planters, that their slaves were escaping into Ohio and were there aided by Ohio citizens to make their escape into Canada. This bill declared that no negro or mulatto should be allowed to settle in the

―――
* The census for this year gives three slaves in Ohio, one each from Muskingum, Lawrence and Preble counties. I have never found any explanation for this strange statement. It seems probable that the census collector believed that once a slave, always a slave, and knowing the three negroes to have been runaways, reported them as slaves.

State unless he could furnish certificates from some court in the United States of his actual freedom.* The same law also enjoined that all blacks who were already residents in the State should register before the first of the following June, with the names of their children, in the records of the county clerk. The fee for registering was 12½ cents per name. This device of the Legislature of 1804 to restrict the immigration of free negroes reminds us of the attempt made by modern legislators to employ the same device against the unwelcome Chinese, and the measures were attended with about the same results in both instances.

Still further to increase the heavy burden of the colored immigrant, it was made a penal offense to employ a negro for one hour unless he could present a certificate of freedom, and any violator of this law should be fined not less than $10 nor more than $50. The same penalty was attached to the humane act of harboring or hindering the capture of a fugitive slave, and for aiding his escape from the State the same should be fined $1,000; the informer thereof usually received one-half the fine, thus placing a premium on spying and tale-bearing, and there were never wanting unscrupulous men ready to testify against anyone who might employ a negro, for the sake of the reward. Besides his fine the would-be friend of the fugitive slave must pay to his owner 50 cents per day for his service. While there was even at this early day a considerable element in the population who were friendly to the negro and would gladly have helped him to earn an honest living in a free State, yet the risks were so great, which must

* Act passed January 5, 1804. Laws of Ohio, 2:63.

be incurred, that they prevented many from rendering the assistance they would otherwise have done.

These are the main provisions of the Act of 1804. I have dwelt upon them somewhat at length because it was the first statute respecting the negro enacted by the Legislature of Ohio, and laid the foundation for the notorious " Black Laws." The same spirit which inspired the Act of 1804 inspired nearly every other act on the subject from that time till 1849. In 1807, to more effectually discourage negro immigration, the law of 1804 was so amended that (*a*) no negro should be allowed to settle in Ohio unless he could within twenty days give bonds to the amount of $500 signed by two bondsmen, who should guarantee his good behavior and support. (*b*) The fine for harboring or concealing a fugitive was raised from $50 to $100, one-half to go to the informer and one-half to the overseer of the poor in the district. (*c*) The proposition made in the constitutional convention (1802), to prohibit negro evidence against a white person, was revived, and it became a statute law of the State of Ohio that no negro should be allowed to give evidence in any case where a white man was a party.* This law worked incalculable mischief to the negroes. It put them at the mercy of unscrupulous white men. A white man could rob, beat and kill a colored man, and unless some white person was present he could escape all punishment. A case is recorded where a white man escaped conviction of murder where there were eight colored eye witnesses, simply because sufficient testimony

———

*Act of January 25, 1807.   Laws of Ohio, 5:53.

of white men could not be found.* Occasions are not wanting where this law " boomeranged" to the injury of the whites themselves. For instance, in 1846 a white man lost his suit against a black man for the payment of a note, for the reason that the only witness which he could introduce in evidence was objected to on account of his color. The judge in pronouncing his decision said: " Let a man be Christian or infidel, let him be Turk or Jew or Mohammedan, let him be sunk to the lowest depths of degradation, he may be a witness in court if he is not black ; the truth shall not be received from a black man when a white man is the party."†

In regard to the general utility of the law the judge further said, " In all my experience, both at the bar and as a member of this court, I cannot recall a single case in which this law has been subservient to the ends of justice."‡

The provision in this law requiring colored settlers to give bonds was, as far as I can learn, a dead letter till 1829, when the trustees of Cincinnati, alarmed at the increasing colored population, issued a proclamation ordering the colored to comply with the requirements of the law within thirty days or leave the city. They petitioned and obtained from the authorities an extension of thirty days. In the meantime they sent a deputation to Canada to ascertain what provision could be made for them there. Before their return the sixty days expired ; finding that few if any had given security, and that the authorities had made no

---

*Proceedings of Ohio Anti-Slavery Convention held at Putnam, 1835, p. 21.

†Jordan vs. Smith. Ohio Reports, 14:201.

‡Idem, p. 204.

effort to enforce the law, some of the citizens became
exasperated and resolved upon forcible expulsion.
The fury of the mob raged for three days and nights.
In vain the colored people besought the authorities
for protection, and at last barricaded their homes and
defended themselves.   Several of their assailants
were killed and wounded, and at length the mob re-
tired.   The deputation from Canada soon returned
with favorable news.   Sir James Colebrook, Governor of Upper Canada, said he would extend to
them a cordial welcome, and "Tell the Republicans
on your side of the line that we royalists do not
know *men* by their color.   Should you come to us
you will be entitled to all the privileges of the rest of
His Majesty's subjects."   On receipt of this intelligence it is estimated that one-half of the colored
population of Cincinnati, numbering about 2,200, left
the city and founded a settlement in Canada, which
they called Wilberforce.*

After the passage of the law of 1807 above mentioned, the political status of the negro remained substantially the same for the next forty-two years.   Colored immigration was discouraged as much as possible, and yet every year an increasing number of free
negroes, or emancipated slaves from the South,
crossed the Ohio river, hoping to find a home in a
free State.   They came to find that the law required
a certificate of freedom and a bond guaranteeing
their good behavior and support before they were
even allowed to settle in the State.   It must however
be said to the honor of Ohio that this law was
observed more in its breach than in compliance

*Proceedings of Ohio Anti-Slavery Convention, held at Putnam
in 1835, p. 19–20.

with it. From all this we see that if the negro settler
was maltreated, robbed or injured in any way by his
white neighbor, there was no redress open to him. If
he would avenge his wrongs he must do it by retalia-
tion, and return the offense in its own kind. He found
the courts closed to him if a white man, however great
a scoundrel, was the aggressor. If white blood flowed
in his veins a man could outrage a negro to his
"heart's content" and be perfectly safe from punishment, if a black man was the only available witness
against him. In only one case would the law accept
the oath of a black man against the testimony of a
white one. The Supreme court decided that in case
of a note for debt a black man might swear to his own
signature, otherwise any white person could forge
his name and the black man would be entirely at his
mercy, since no one could sware to his plea but himself.* With this single exception, the colored settler
in Ohio found himself in the hands of his white
neighbors. If he was indicted for crime, his cause
must come before a jury composed entirely of white
men who, as a rule, were already prejudiced against
him on account of his color. By a law passed as
early as 1824, and again in 1828 and 1831, black
men were excluded from ever serving as jurymen.†
Even the privilege of shouldering his musket in defence of his white neighbor's country was denied
the colored patriot, for the militia as well as the jury
was closed to any one who had more African than
Caucasian blood.‡ If he would redress his wrongs
at the polls, he found the ballot, too, was not his to

* Ohio Reports; Jordan vs. Smith, vol. 14, p. 199 seq.
† Laws of Ohio, 26:43 and 29:94.
‡ Laws of Ohio, 2:5.

use. His property could be taxed, his own status fixed by an assembly which he had no voice in electing, no matter how light his complexion, and many times it was fairer than the white voter's; the ballot was refused him if he was even suspected of being a black man. By judicial decision in 1842, the term "white" was interpreted as comprehending all persons having more white than colored blood.* In

In consequence of this interpretation, a few octaroons in the State were enfranchised, but of course the great majority of negroes were of pure, or nearly pure, African blood and were not affected by this decision. It is very clear that the negro in Ohio possessed only a quasi-legal position; in fact, it was explicitly stated in a law passed 1829, providing for the maintenance of the "poor," that nothing in the act should be so construed as to permit a black or mulatto person to gain a legal settlement in the State.†

The laws mentioned above, restricting and determining the condition of the negro in the State, together with the laws excluding him from the public schools, the details of which will be given in the following chapter, were collectively styled the "Black Laws" of Ohio, and under that name became notorious throughout the country. By their injustice and cruelty they established for the State an extremely unenviable reputation. With all her boast of freedom, of her inheritance of the Ordinance of 1787, and of her honorable descent from the North-

---

* Ohio Reports, Jeffries vs. Ankery, 11:372 seq. This decision was confirmed the following year in the case of Lane vs. Baker et al., Ohio Reports, 12:2373 seq., and again in case of Anderson vs. Milliken, Ohio State Reports, 9:568.

†Passed February 12, 1829. Laws of Ohio, 27:35.

west territory, it was said to her shame that the
slave States themselves treated their free colored
population with scarcely more cruelty than did the
free State of Ohio.*

The more considerate and humane people were
aroused at such criticism upon their fair State, and
demanded a revision if not a repeal of these iniquitous laws. They boldly declared that their blackness
should no longer obscure the brightness of Ohio's
standing among the States of the Union. The only
agency through which this could be accomplished
was that of the great political parties. Of the two,
the Whig party had always been regarded as being
more disposed to be just and charitable in its treatment of the negro inhabitants than the Democratic,
but in 1848 the Whigs nominated and elected a
Southern slave holder for President of the United
States. In despair of obtaining anything from their
old, venerated party, many forsook its lines and cast
their lot with the Free-Soil party. Many others
were undecided which way to turn. Had the Demo-

---

* The following poem was composed by M. C. Sampson, a
colored man, which probably expressed the opinion of many colored people regarding Ohio:

> Ohio's not the place for me;
> For I was much surprised
> So many of her sons to see
> In garments of disguise.
> Her name has gone out through the world,
> Free labor—soil—and man—
> But slaves had better far be hurled
> Into the lion's den.
> Farewell, Ohio!
> I cannot stop in thee;
> I'll travel on to Canada,
> Where colored men are free.

Taken from a collection of negro songs.

cratic party come out squarely on an anti-slavery
platform it would no doubt have carried with it the
wavering, Whigs and many Free-Soilers. But to
such a course it was not prepared and could not be
expected to commit itself. The times, however,
were ripe for some movement toward the ameliora-
tion of the condition of the colored people in Ohio.
The vote of colored sympathizers was no longer so
insignificant as to be wisely ignored. The Free-Soil
party held the balance of power and was in a situation to compel concessions from either of the other
parties. As we have already mentioned, the "Black
Laws" had long been notorious throughout the
country, and many and threatening were the anathemas hurled against them by anti-slavery speakers.
During the Presidential campaign of 1848 William
H. Seward, in a vigorous political speech delivered
at Cleveland, urged upon the parents of Ohio to
inculcate the laws of freedom and equal rights of
man, under the paternal roof, and to see to it that
they were taught in the schools and churches. And
referring more particularly to the Black Laws he
said, "Reform your code, extend a cordial welcome
to the fugitive who lays his weary limbs at your
door, and defend him as you would your paternal
gods; correct your errors that slavery has any constitutional guarantee which may not be released, and
ought to be relinquished—say to slavery when it
shows its 'bond' and demands its 'pound of flesh,'
that if it draws one drop of blood its life shall be
forfeit." *   Speeches like this so aroused the Free-
Soilers that they resolved to make a determined effort
to blot out from the statute books of Ohio the dis-

* Speech at Cleveland, October 26, 1848. Seward's Works, 3:301.

graceful discriminations against the colored people. The composition of the General Assembly in the following year (1849) was such as offered an especially favorable opportunity for such a movement. In the House there were thirteen Free-Soilers and eleven Whigs—Free-Soilers, that is, Whigs with pronounced anti-slavery convictions, and who generally affiliated with the Free-Soil party when no important political question was at stake. If the regular "Old Line Whigs," as they were called, together with the Whig-Free-Soilers, would cast a solid vote, they could just tie the vote of the "Old Line Democrats." Besides these elements there were in the House two Independents, as they called themselves, Messrs. Morse of Lake county and Townshend of Lorain. These two had generally affiliated themselves with the Free-Soilers, but by refusing to bind themselves to support all legislation proposed by the Free-Soilers they had been read out of the party. As a consequence the balance of power was substantially thrown into the hands of these two men. They quickly perceived their advantage, and were prepared to give their vote only to that party which promised to support the measure which they championed. They were both strong anti-slavery men, and were equally pronounced in their sympathies for the free colored people of Ohio. The "Black Laws" comprehended three general divisions of legislative action :

1.—The prohibition against negroes settling in the State, unless a certificate of freedom could be shown and bonds given, guaranteeing good behavior and support.

2.—The disqualification of the negro to testify in

courts where a white man was a party, or to serve as juryman.

3.—The exclusion of the negroes from the advantages of the public schools.

To secure the repeal of these laws was the one task which Morse and Townshend set themselves to accomplish; a task which had been the cherished object of the Free-Soil party from its first organization was finally effected by these same two men whom, in their narrow-mindedness, they had read out of their party. The actual repeal was the outcome of a bargain made between the Democratic and Free-Soil party, in the following manner.

It was the year for the election of a United States Senator from Ohio, and a vacancy on the bench of the Supreme Court was to be filled. The contest between the parties chiefly centered in these two interests. The Free-Soil candidate for Senator was Joshua R. Giddings, who was a personal friend of Mr. Morse, and was warmly supported by him, while Mr. Townshend as earnestly favored Salmon P. Chase, but both were more anxious for the repeal of the " Black Laws" than for the election of any particular favorite of their own. It was agreed that Morse should propose to the Whigs that if they would vote for the repeal act and for the election of Joshua R. Giddings as Senator, these two Independents (Morse and Townshend) would give their votes to the Whig candidate for the Supreme Court. But the Whigs thought that to accept Giddings, with his Free-Soil notions, was too big a price to pay, and so refused the proposition. A similar proposition was made by Townshend to the Democrats, with merely the substitution of Chase for Giddings.

Chase had for years subordinated all political action
to that of " detaching the Federal Government from
any and all responsibility for human slavery."*
And with the conviction that the " Old Line Democrats" would come up to the standard of the Independents, Chase had acted with them ;† for this
reason the proposal of Townshend was not altogether
disagreeable to the Democratic members of the
House, and the agreement was made. A bill was
at once drawn up by Chase to repeal the "Black
Laws" and to provide for the education of colored
children. The bill was introduced into the House
by Mr. Morse, and carried by a large majority. In
the Senate the bill was referred to a committee, who
moved an amendment exempting from repeal laws
prohibiting colored people from a place on the jury
and from admittance to poor houses. The bill as
amended was finally passed, February 10, 1849.‡

From this time there was a marked change in the
sentiment of the people regarding the negro. As

*Schuckers' Life of Chase, p. 95.

†Schuckers' Life of Chase, p. 95. In my account of the repeal
of the Black Laws I have followed an article on the subject by
N. S. Townshend in the Ohio Historical and Archæological Quar-
terly, 1, p. 130, with references to Schuckers' Chase, p. 95 seq., for
confirmation, and some additional information. The acts repealed
were those of Jan. 5, 1804, Laws of Ohio 46:81; Jan. 3, 1807,
Laws of Ohio 2:63; Feb. 27, 1839, Laws of Ohio 5:53; Feb. 27,
1848, Laws of Ohio 37:38; "and all parts of other acts, so far as
they enforce any disabilities or convey any privileges on account
of color," excepting acts of Feb. 9, 1839 (Laws of Ohio 29:94)
excluding colored men from jury service, and act of March 14,
1831 (Laws of Ohio 29:320) providing for the relief of the poor,
which enjoined that nothing in the act should be construed,
as enabling any black person to gain a legal settlement in the
State, and thus be entitled to any benefit from the "poor laws."

‡Laws of Ohio, 47:17.

soon as they were given a legal standing in the
courts they were treated more as men. There was,
however, but little disposition to grant them suffrage,
and still less to treat them as social equals, and
admittance to the public schools was still denied, yet
very many privileges and rights as citizens were
extended to them. By the same act, repealing the
"Black Laws," separate schools for colored children
were established. Thus the free colored man at
home shared in the general sympathy which began
to be expressed for his less fortunate brothers in
bondage. The tide of public prejudice, which had
so long deprived him and his children of the rights
and protection of law, was now slowly receding, and
Ohio was beginning to rank as a strong anti-slavery
State.

The Constitution of the State was the same as
when it was admitted in 1802. The growth of
the State in wealth and population, together with the
introduction of steam and electricity, had occasioned
so many radical changes in the economic and social
life of the State that many legal questions had arisen
which were quite unforseen, and hence unprovided
for in 1802. So the year after the "Repeal Act"
was passed, while Congress was struggling over the
question of slavery extension in the proposed State
of California, and the acceptance of the great compromise of 1850, with the notorious Fugitive Slave
Law as a distinctive feature, Ohio was struggling
over a revision of its Constitution. To this end a
convention convened in Columbus, May 6, 1850, and
from the first day the question of the status of the
negro in the State was made prominent in the delib-
erations of the convention. The greatest diversity

of opinion existed among its members ; some were willing to allow him every legal privilege accorded the white man, some would deprive him of those already possessed, while others would drive him from the State altogether, and forever bar the doors against negro immigration.

From every part of the State were presented petitions, representing every shade of opinion on the subject, one praying to extend, the other to restrict, until, in a bewildering maze of conflicting sentiments, it was hard to determine which " horn of the dilemma " had the greater power. The discussions in the convention upon the actual status of the negro might naturally be classified under five heads : (1) Extradition and immigration. (2) State aid and colonization. (3) Employment of colored men in militia service. (4) The extension of the elective franchise. (5) The admission of colored children to the public schools. Two and five will be considered in later chapters. As early as the third day of the convention, a memorial was presented from the citizens of Lorain and Hardin counties, praying the convention to authorize the State Legislature to pass an act for the extradition of colored people in the State. At the time of its being presented, the memorial elicited no discussion, but no little debate followed upon the propriety of printing the petition. It was finally decided to print it, and thus was established a precedent for receiving and printing anti-slavery petitions, which it was found difficult to break down, as later some of the members were disposed to do, when the question came up as to the reception and disposition of pro-negro memorials. Petitions asking for extradition or for laws prohibiting colored immigration continued to pour in upon the convention. As many as three were received in one day.* Those petitioners who desired prohibition of immigration generally asked that the law denying to negroes the right of testifying in a case where whites were party, be revived and embodied in the Constitution, or in the statute laws of the State. Proposals for State aid to colonization were sometimes coupled with these petitions. From no less eminent source than Daniel Drake, who has contributed so much valuable information on the pioneer history of Ohio, came a petition to the effect that the entrance into the State both of emancipated and fugitive slaves be prohibited, and that laws be enacted favoring African colonization, and out of respect to Mr. Drake it was laid on the table and ordered printed.† From Battle county a memorial was received, signed by 135 citizens, praying that colored people be removed from the State, but desiring it to be done with " prudence and humanity "— that they should not be " deprived of their property without proper compensation." ‡ These petitions reveal the extreme anti-negro sentiments held by many in the State. This feeling, as has been said before, was strongest in the southern counties bordering on the Ohio river, as the population here was largely from the South, who, from birth and education, or from social and business relations, were heartily in sympathy with their old home interests and institutions, and most naturally cherished a

---

* June 17, one each from Jefferson, Brown and Hamilton counties.

† Debates Ohio Convention 1850, 2:158.

‡ Debates Ohio Convention, 1850, 2:191.

strong antipathy for the negro, whether free or slave, who found a home in Ohio. These colored settlers along the river simply eked out a pitiful existence, by working in boats and around the docks, doing odd jobs here and there, as occasion offered or necessity demanded. While there was at this time quite a population of Quakers in the river towns, with most pronounced anti-slavery principles and earnest sympathies for the oppressed, yet the large majority of the whites, confounding the man with his condition, regarded the negro as despicable and wanted him removed from the State limits. With such a strong public prejudice against him it is not surprising that nearly every petition presented to the convention, praying for the extradition or prohibition of immigration of colored people, should have emanated from the southern counties.

In the northern part of the State the circumstances were very different. The population here was largely from the Eastern States, who came with few inherent prejudices against the negro, no life-long associations with him, nor as great commercial interests connected with him. The few negroes who had settled in the rural districts manifested much more ambition and capacity for getting a living than those along the river. They cultivated small farms, and generally secured the confidence of their white neighbors. But the convention represented the interests of the whole State, and, as a rule, stood ready to receive all petitions, on any subject whatever, which were sent to it. We find that those praying for extradition were usually laid on the table, with the tacit understanding that they would not be taken up again ; while those asking for prohibition of negro immigration were generally referred to the Committee on Bill of Rights, and were never heard from again, and yet these petitions were not without their effect.   There were really many members who were favorably disposed toward them and would have rejoiced to have had their prayers answered, and through them one serious effort was made to prohibit further negro immigration, and to secure State aid for colonization.   A motion to that effect was amended as follows :   " The General Assembly shall by law prohibit black or mulatto persons from emigrating into or becoming residents within the limits of the State."*   This amendment was greeted with a storm of indignation.   Many who were opposed to conferring the electoral franchise upon the negro were not disposed to deny him an asylum, where he could at least be suffered to live.   Mr. W. S. Bates, of Jefferson county, most vigorously denounced the amendment.   He said :   " We proudly boast that our country is the asylum of the poor and oppressed of all nations—our invitations are wafted on every breeze ;   and reaching the recesses of human degradation, have lighted up the visions of hope to millions who were ready to perish ; and the floods of emigration are still surging with the continual out-pourings of Europe.   But here is a down-trodden race emphatically the victim of oppression, not *foreigners*, but *natives* of the United States, and they *alone* are to be prohibited from setting their feet on our soil."†   On other grounds than those of justice and humanity was the amendment opposed.   The assertion of such a clause in the Constitution would be not only highly

---

* Debates of Convention, 2:598.
† Debates of the Convention, 1850, 2:600.

inexpedient, but would practically rehabilitate the " Black Laws " in an even more obnoxious and sweeping form than when they were repealed by an almost unanimous vote. It would not only be in direct opposition to the already expressed public sentiment, but would throw upon the people the alternative of accepting the Constitution with the obnoxious clause attachment, or of rejecting it altogether. This would be not merely a breach of faith on the part of the Convention, but would greatly endanger the chances for its ratification. The opposition to the amendment continued to grow so great that Mr. Holmes of Hamilton county, who had offered the motion, finally asked and obtained leave to withdraw it, and so the question never came to a vote, and we have no means of ascertaining how many of the members really favored it. A modified form of the original motion was again proposed, praying that the General Assembly, with such appropriate legislation as would be consistent with the Constitution of the United States, should " discourage the immigration of colored people into the State." On this second proposition a division was called for, and the vote stood 39 for and 58 against.* This is probably not very different from what it would have been on the first.

No further effort was made to interfere directly with colored immigration. It was found quite impracticable as well as inhuman to dislodge the negro who had already established himself in the State, and equally impracticable as well as impolitic to prohibit his coming in the future.

---

* Debates, 2:604.

3. MILITIA SERVICE.

The negro in Ohio had never been called upon to perform military service. There had always been a pronounced opposition to put firearms into their hands. This, no doubt, arose from the constant fear in the South of slave uprisings ; there it was made a penal offense for a slave to be found with firearms in his possession. For this reason and for the fact that military service was generally held to be more of a duty than a privilege, the friends of the negro in the convention did not vigorously contest the report of the committee providing the establishment of a State militia.* Nevertheless, when the article was read, Mr. Townsend, the champion of negro rights, at once moved to strike out the word "white." It is probable that he had but little faith in the success of his motion, but he never allowed an opportunity to escape him to advance the interests of the colored people ; as he no doubt anticipated, the motion was lost by a vote of 22 to 62. It may not be difficult to appreciate the opposition to negro suffrage and to the attendance of colored children at white schools, but it is difficult to understand what could be the objection to permitting him to shoulder a gun in defense of his State and country. There was not wanting precedent for this. In the War of the Revolution negroes were enlisted for active service, and General Jackson, in the second war with England, at Mobile, September 21, 1814, issued a proclamation to all free colored inhabitants of Louisiana to rally to the defense of their country, promising them the same bounty which was awarded to white

*Ohio Constitution, Art. ix., Sec. 1. All white male citizens shall . . . be enrolled in the militia and perform military duty. . .

soldiers. To this call they responded with a heroism worthy of any race, be it African or Caucasian, and conducted themselves in such a manly and efficient fashion that General Jackson publicly thanked them for their services and said they had surpassed his hopes, and that the President of the United States would be informed of their bravery.*

It is doubtful whether many of the members of the Convention of 1850 or their constituents knew of Jackson's Proclamation of 1814, and it is still more doubtful if it would have made any difference in their action if they had known. Men are not easily influenced by precedent when prejudice is already formed and holds them fast. A careful study of the debates on this point, in the convention, reveals at least four pretty well defined reasons which governed the members in their objections to enrolling the negroes in the militia service.

1.   There was a disposition, as far as possible, to ignore the presence of the negro in the State, and to this end, deprive him of all privileges and duties as a citizen, save that only of paying taxes.

2.   The arming of the negro would be horrifying to the South, especially Virginia and Kentucky, and this consideration was strong enough to determine the votes of the delegates from the Southern counties.

3.   The fearful consequences of training to arms an ever-increasing, non-privileged class in the State created "a shudder when they reflected that God is just," and that the possibility of a negro uprising might not be limited to slave territory.

4.   The admission of the negro to military service

*Proclamation can be found in Niles' Register, 7:205.

would necessitate, in drilling and in camp life, an association with the whites, which would be extremely repugnant. The companies of the militia were somewhat of a social organization and the presence of the black man would destroy their companionable character.

For these reasons, in part at least, the negroes were exempted from military duty by the convention, and the subject never came up again in the legislative councils of the State till the Civil War, when they themselves petitioned for the privilege of defending themselves, their families and their country from the invasion of their Southern neighbors.

4.   ELECTIVE FRANCHISE.

The greatest contest of the convention, as far as the negro was concerned, was waged over the question of negro suffrage.   The convention was nearly smothered with petitions asking that the same civic privileges be extended to the black man as were accorded to the white.   On the same day* that the first petition was presented praying for the removal of the colored people from the State, the discussion of which question we have already considered (under the head of Extradition and Immigration), one from the citizens of Stark and Columbiana counties was laid before the convention, praying that equal rights be granted the whole people without regard to color or sex.   This petition appeared to excite no special interest, and it was about to be referred to the appropriate committee, when William Sawyer, a blacksmith representing Auglaize county, arose and in most unequivocal terms announced himself as op-

* May 8.

posed to receiving the petition. He said "he felt
constrained by a sense of duty to his constituents to
say, here and now, he would not sit still and permit
even his fellow citizens to petition that negroes should
be entitled to all the privileges and immunities of
white men, without raising his voice against it, and
accordingly he moved the question of the petition."
It is difficult to see on what ground Sawyer could
accuse himself of dereliction of duty in receiving a
courteously worded petition from the citizens of Ohio.
But from the first he assumed to himself the special
duty of trying to thwart every effort made for the advancement of the colored people.

Two days later a similar petition was again presented. Mr. Sawyer was upon his feet in an instant,
protesting against the propriety of the convention
consuming so much time in receiving such communi-
cations and in allowing them to be made. But the
right of petition was vigorously defended. Many
who were opposed to the prayer of the petition stood
firm against any encroachment on the right of the
people to petition and to demand a courteous reception of their petitions at the hands of the convention.*
The question of receiving the petition being put, it
was resolved in the affirmative by a vote of 101 to 2.
The precedent thus established, there was no serious
objection again offered to the reception of petitions
of this character. Occasionally one would elicit
some sarcastic ejaculation, and a spirited debate
would follow. One such case occurred which
aroused much harsh criticism and bad feeling among
the Abolitionists and friends of the negro throughout
the State. A petition for equal rights drew out the

* Debates Convention, 1:58.

remark that it were better to allow all such "effusions of folly and fanaticism to go to the table as quickly as possible." The remark was widely circulated by the newspapers, and aroused a great deal of bitter feeling; and when a few days later a member insinuatingly asked whether a certain petition, presented in behalf of the negroes, was couched in respectful language, the friends of the colored people were fired with indignation. A few weeks later another petition for negro suffrage was presented by the citizens of Ashtabula county, and was accompanied by a letter to their representative, Mr. Hunter, in which it was suggested that it would be well for the convention to remember its obligations to the people and not characterize their petition as an "ebullition of folly and fanaticism." Mr. Hunter, in presenting the petition, said that "he was in hearty accord with the suggestions of the letter," and remarked further that it seemed to him rather singular that an assembly which so often spoke of themselves as emanating from the people, and who called themselves the *servants* of the people, and the people their *masters* and *sovereigns*, should so often indulge in insinuating and disrespectful language toward the people, while they were so very sensitive at the discovery of the least disrespect on the part of the people.*

But all this was merely preliminary skirmishing. The battle really began when the committee on Elective Franchise brought in their report, December 4. The clause which they had drafted conferred the privilege of franchise only on "white male citizens." It was immediately moved to strike out the word "white," for the reason that negroes were made

* Debates Convention, 1:337.

amenable to the law, and it was just and expedient
that they should have a voice in making laws. No
decision was taken at that time, and further consideration of the report was postponed.* Two months
passed before the question was again taken up. At
that time, Mr. Townshend, who was a member of the
committee, desired to make a minority report, but
the rules of the convention did not allow minority
reports to be accompanied by the reasons for them,
consequently Townshend offered his objections to the
report independently of his position on the committee.
Of course he was strongly opposed to the presence
of the word "white," and sustained his objection on
the ground that such limitation was unjust, anti-
democratic, impolitic and ambiguous.† Mr. Townshend made a strong plea for negro suffrage, but he
made the mistake so frequently done by the advocates of extensive suffrage, viz., that of confusing
right and privilege. To vote is a privilege granted
by the State to certain of its members, but no one
can demand it as an inherent right. The many
vagaries about the "inherent rights of man" which
were entertained and popularized by French phil-
osophical writers and which the Revolution spread
broad-cast over the world, have always affected the
thought and speech of American statesmen. There
is no question, however, that the monopoly of suffrage claimed for the "white male citizens" was
anti-democratic, and though it may not always follow that it was impolitic, yet in the case of the negro
in Ohio at that time this enfranchisement could not
have been attended with any great evils. The

* Debates Convention, 2:8.
† Debates of Convention, 2:635.

privilege and responsibility of the ballot would
no doubt have awakened the more manly instincts
in the negro and have inspired him to attain a
greater intellectual and moral elevation, and as a
consequence he would have become a more
patriotic and capable citizen, and been stirred
to a more active and progressive life. The argument
for enfranchisement, on the ground that the term
"white" was ambiguous, has more force in it than
may appear at first sight. There were many among
the colored people of Ohio who were by race and
descent negroes, but who in complexion were as fair
or fairer than their white neighbors. Judges in
elections had often experienced great difficulty in
deciding whether the applicant was actually a white
man, and thus a legal voter, or not, and a blunder
here on the part of the judges would arouse a general
indignation and the bitter resentment of the offended
party. Through their representative, Mr. Hunter,
twenty citizens of Ashtabula county sent a petition
to the convention, asking that some uniform method
might be determined upon, which should guide the
election judges in deciding the color of a man desiring to vote. Mr. Hunter said, "The only object of
the petition was to protest against the ridiculousness
of such a variable, uncertain and whimsical method
as was now in use for determining the qualifications
necessary to secure the elective franchise."* But
there was so little disposition on the part of many of the
members to extend suffrage to the negro, that no
amount of argument would have convinced them of
its expediency; they greatly preferred to ignore the
presence of the colored population in Ohio, and to

* Debates of Convention, 2:614.

draft a Constitution with no reference to them whatever. But twenty-five thousand people, backed up
by numerous and persistent friends, would not suffer
themselves to be ignored ; they demanded a hearing,
and the convention was obliged to listen and to give
them a definite answer.

The convention, as a whole, was disposed to give
the subject as fair and impartial a consideration as
could have been expected in an assembly of that
character. The speakers who championed the negro
cause manifested great moderation, breadth of mind
and a good common sense. Their speeches were
remarkably free from the fanaticism and narrow-
mindedness which characterized so many of the
early Abolitionists. They treated their opponents
with a courtesy which was not always reciprocated.
Those members who would forever shut the doors of
the State against the colored people, and were always
ready to accept any accusation against them, and
who improved every opportunity to present any
argument, however false and foolish, which might
work against their cause, could not be expected to
give any great consideration to those who radically
differed from them on this subjuct. It was a favorite
fancy with the extremists that the United States was
especially set apart by the great Creater to be the
home of the white man, and it would be contrary to
the divine design to give the negro any part or lot
within its boundaries. They had apparently overlooked or forgotten the fact that the negro was first
brought here by the white man, and by his laws had
been compelled to stay here. The real sentiment
of the majority of the members of the convention, on
the question of negro enfranchisement, was probably

pretty accurately expressed by Mr. Nash, delegate
from Gallia. He opposed the extension of suffrage
for the very valid reason that it was not in accord
with public opinion, and that it would prevent the
ratification of the Constitution.* This was no doubt
true. Though there was a large and continually
increasing element in the State who favored negro
suffrage, yet the vast majority of voters would have
cast their ballots against it. This view is confirmed
by the fact that as late as 1867, when the question
was directly submitted to the people in the form of an
amendment, it was defeated by over 50,000 majority,
and to have adopted it then would have been to send
the Constitution before the people with its own death
warrant attached. The risk of such a calamity the
convention could not afford to take, and consequently when the division was called on the motion
to strike out the word "white," it was resolved in
the negative by the almost unanimous vote of 12
to 66. A motion to amend by authorizing the General Assembly, in case it was deemed expedient, to
"extend the suffrage to inhabitants of the State not
hereby qualified as electors," was defeated by an
equally large majority. Thus the negro was
definitely excluded from any participation in the
political life of the State. One privilege was, however, permitted him. In taking the census, upon
which depended the appointment of legislative representation, he was never excluded. Even the southern county members, who had been the strongest
opponents to their enfranchisement, had no objection
to counting them as citizens, when by so doing an
increase of representatives would be gained from

---

* Debates of Convention, 2:553.

their respective counties. The apportionment was made by dividing the "whole population" by the number one hundred.* A similar provision was made concerning the appointment for Senators. In this respect the framers of the Constitution of 1802 were more consistent than those of 1850-1851, for they counted in the census for apportionment only actual voters, that is, the white male inhabitants above twenty-one years of age.† The political status of the negro, as determined by the revised Constitution, was not materially changed till the passage of the Fifteenth Amendment opened up to him the right to participate in all legal privileges enjoyed by the white man. In respect to the question of slavery, there was no disposition on the part of the convention to alter any regulations established by the Ordinance of 1787, and afterwards incorporated in the Constitution of 1802, and subsequently embodied in that of 1850, excepting that the provision regarding indenture was omitted.‡

To the better understanding of the change of public sentiment which soon followed regarding the educa-

---

* Ohio Constitution, 1850-1851, Art. xi., Sec. 1. The apportion of this State for members of the General Assembly shall be made every ten years in the following manner : The *whole population* of the State, as ascertained by the Federal courts, . . . shall be divided by the number 100 . . . The ratio for Senators shall forever hereafter be ascertained by dividing the whole population of the State by thirty-five.

† Ohio Constitution of 1802, Art. i., Sec. 2. . . . "The number of representatives . . . shall be fixed by Legislature and apportioned among the several counties according to the number of white male inhabitants above twenty-one years of age."

‡ Ohio Constitution of 1850-1851, Art. i., Sec. 6. There shall be no slavery in this State, nor involuntary servitude, unless for the punishment of crime. This clause was incorporated into the revised Constitution of 1873.

tion of the negro, I wish to add in this connection (a
more detailed account will be given in a subsequent
chapter), that although the friends of the negro failed
to secure the adoption of a clause into the Constitution admitting colored children to the public schools,
they did succeed so far as to have an article providing for the establishment of common schools to be so
worded as not to exclude them, and to leave the
question to the discretion of the General Assembly.
Public sentiment in all parts of the State was not yet
ready to allow the intermingling of colored children with the white in common schools. It did
recognize the necessity for the education of the colored children, and we find that provision was made
for separate schools, by an act of Legislature in
1853.* The Constitution as revised by the Convention of 1850 was ratified by the people and
continued in force till 1873, when the changes
occasioned by the Civil War made it necessary to
again revise it in order to accommodate itself to the
changed circumstances. As we have shown, the
Convention of 1850 had not materially altered the
political condition of the negro, either for better or
for worse, but the question, of his rights and privileges had been most thoroughly discussed, and thereby
his cause had been really advanced. The ranks of
his friends had been largely increased, their sympathy
and enthusiasm in his behalf had been greatly
strengthened, and as a consequence he was in a much
better position to secure more favorable laws in the future and ultimately to obtain political equality. During
ten years before the Civil War the anti-slavery feeling
d become predominant in the State, and Ohio in

---

*Laws of Ohio, 51:441.

common with other States passed a "Personal Liberty Law" prohibiting the use of the State and county jails for the confinement of fugitive slaves.* It ·was also enacted that if any one should arrest or detain a person under the pretense that the same was a fugitive from justice, he would be considered guilty of false imprisonment.† Both of these laws were repealed in less than one year, and neither of them of course effected the free colored population of the State ; they were only the result of an outburst of indignation against the operation of the iniquitous fugitive slave law, consequently as soon as that some what subsided, the laws were repealed. The history of Ohio had always furnished two parties in the anti-slavery discussion, one moderate and charitable, the other impetuous and bitter ; one disposed to be lenient toward their Southern neighbors, the other keenly alert toward the slightest encroachment of the slavocracy, and untiring in their efforts to aid its victims. If these divisions of sentiment could have presented an untiring front against the enemy, their power and influence would have increased in a corresponding ratio.

Coming down to the beginning of the war, we find the people of Ohio intensely loyal to the Union and ready as of old to "pledge their lives, their fortunes and their sacred honor" in its defense. However, had the emancipation of the slaves been the issue at the first, it is exceedingly doubtful if the call for volunteers would have met with such abun-

---

*Passed April 16, 1857. Laws of Ohio, 54:170. Repealed February 25, 1858. Laws of Ohio, 55:10.

†Passed April 17, 1857. Laws of Ohio, 54:186. Repealed March 27, 1858. Laws of Ohio, 55:19.

dant response as it did. The question of intermarriage of the races came up during the first year of
the war, and aroused the deepest interest. There
had been an occasional instance of the kind, and
fears were entertained that unless the laws forbid it
the practice might become common.

Accordingly, January 31, 1861, a law was passed
"to prevent the amalgamation of the white and colored races."* I think it is generally conceded that
the law was a wise one, though the necessity for it
is not always so obvious, for there seemed to be very
little disposition then, as now, to intermarry. Notwithstanding the races are now legally equal, yet
social prejudices still continue, and it is extremely
doubtful if they ever will be wholly obliterated ; till
the last vestige of race feeling has become extinct,
and social as well as political equality is recognized,
it must be to the advantage of both blacks and
whites that intermarriage be forbidden either by
custom or by law. As it seems quite impossible to
realize social equality without amalgamation, the
time when absolute equality will be attained seems
infinitely removed.

During the Civil War, the colored people magnan-
imously overlooked the discrimination which the
State government had made against them, and we
find them intensely patriotic and eager to enlist in
the State troops. To this effect repeated petitions
were presented to Governor Tod and were persist-
ently denied. May 11, 1863, he said, " I do not
propose to raise any colored troops."† Governor
Andrews of Massachusetts was given authority to

* Laws of Ohio, 58:6.
† Tod to Andrews, May 16, 1863.

enlist colored men in any loyal State, and transportation there was paid by the Government, and as a consequence, many colored patriots from Ohio flocked there and joined the Massachusetts troops. Governor Tod encouraged this, and requested Governor Andrews to organize the colored volunteers from Ohio, as far as possible, in separate companies, and to keep a complete list of them.* Not till the efficiency of colored troops was found probable was the United States Government willing to grant the State governors a general permission to raise them ; it watched the result of Governor Andrews' experiment in Massachusetts. May 27, 1863, Secretary Stanton wrote Governor Tod, " If successful in Massachusetts, there will be enough left to give you a regiment or more in Ohio."† It soon became obvious that Ohio was becoming a recruiting ground for Massachusetts. The State government realized this when it found that all available men were needed to fill out the State quota. Application was accordingly made to the United States Government for permission to raise colored companies. When such permission was received, Governor Tod at once issued a proclamation calling for colored volunteers, and established a rendezvous camp at Delaware. Railroads were requested to give transportation to all colored recruits to Delaware, and the 127th O. V. I. (colored) was organized. The pay per month for colored soldiers was fixed at ten dollars, with no provision for the support of their families. Governor Tod, who had now apparently become

---

* Tod to Hon. William Porter, May 11, 1863. Ex. Doc., 1863, Part 1, p. 270.

† Stanton to Tod, May 27, 1863.

enthusiastic over his colored regiment, issued an appeal to the people of the State to raise funds by voluntary subscription for the relief of destitute colored families, who had been bereft of their support.* The name of the regiment was changed to the 5th United States Colored Troops; in consequence, Ohio received credit for only a little over one-third of the colored citizens who really volunteered for the war.† But they all so gallantly conducted themselves that Ohio has just cause to be proud of its colored defenders.‡

While the end of the war brought freedom to the slaves, it did not immediately improve the status of the free colored people in Ohio. The Thirteenth Amendment, abolishing slavery, was, of course, ratified by the Ohio Legislature, without opposition. The action of the General Assembly respecting the Fourteenth Amendment is somewhat curious. Congress proposed this amendment to the States in June, 1866, and in January, 1867, the Assembly in Ohio passed a resolution of ratification.§ But in just one year and three days from that time, the Assembly passed a resolution rescinding their former resolution of ratification.‖ In the midst of this controversy over the Fourteenth Amendment, on April 6, 1867, the Assembly resolved to submit to the people an amendment to the State Constitution granting the right of suffrage to all *male* citizens of above

---

* Appeal issued June 22, 1863.   Ex. Doc., 1863, part 1, p. 274.
† Reid's Ohio in the War, 1:177.
‡ Among the figures which adorn the Soldiers' Monument in Cleveland, dedicated July 4, 1894, is one of a full-blooded African standing beside a white man engaged in loading a cannon.
§ Laws of Ohio, 64:320.
‖ January 15, 1868.   Laws of Ohio, 65:280.

twenty-one years of age.* This action anticipated the proposal of the Fifteenth Amendment by nearly two years, and its results determined the vote of the General Assembly when that amendment was submitted to it.† The people of Ohio, even after the four years' war which secured the emancipation of the slaves, were yet in no humor to grant their own free negroes the right of suffrage.

The proposed amendment to the State Constitution as offered April 6, 1867, was defeated at the October elections, 1867, by the large majority of 50,000. This vote shows very plainly that a large part of the citizens of Ohio had no disposition to acknowledge the negro as a political equal, and entitled to the rights and privileges of the white man.

Two years before this proposed Constitutional amendment, the Ohio Democratic State Convention, which assembled in Columbus August 24, 1865, declared "that the effort now being made to confer the right of suffrage upon negroes was an invidious attempt to overthrow popular institutions, by bringing the right to vote into disgrace."‡ And further declared that if allowed to vote, the negroes would hold the balance of power in State politics, and white demagogues and renegades, by pandering to the negro, would secure control of the State government; and still further, that the white laborer, by negro competition, would soon be reduced to the condition of the Russian serf and "Ohio would become the negro paradise and the white man's wilderness."

* Laws of Ohio, 64:328.

† Fifteenth Amendment proposed by Congress, February 26, 1869.

‡Pamphlet issued in 1865—Negro Suffrage and Equality, p. 15.

On the other hand, there was a large contingent in
the State belonging to the Abolition and Republican
parties, who maintained that equity, justice and expediency demanded the enfranchisement of the negroes ;
but, as we have seen, they were outvoted by a large
majority. In order to render more effective the will
of the people, the Legislature, April 16, 1868, passed
an "Act to Preserve the Purity of Elections." The
object of this law was to minimize as much as possible the negro's chances for casting a vote. The
provisions were very elaborate and numerous. Any
person offering to vote, with the slightest visible
admixture of African blood, was compelled to take a
solemn oath to truthfully answer the questions put to
him. Then followed a long list of questions, whose
object was to elicit a confession that he was a
negro, and if any person secured the right to vote
by false swearing, he was adjudged guilty of perjury
and a sentence of from three to ten years in the
penitentiary followed, while the judge of elections
who received the vote of a negro was liable to six
months' imprisonment in the county jail, and a civil
action might be brought against him to the amount
of $500 by any elector in the county where such
vote was cast.* Such was the law and sentiment
of Ohio respecting negro suffrage when Congress
submitted to the Legislature the Fifteenth Amendment, which prohibited the States from denying or
abridging the right of suffrage " on account of race,
color or previous condition of servitude." The
spirit of this amendment was entirely contrary to the
policy pursued by the State from its formation. In
Constitutional and statute laws the people had repeat-

*Laws of Ohio, 65:97.

edly declared against negro suffrage, and only the
year before they had given a decided expression of
preference not to amend the then existing laws of the
State.

The Fifteenth Amendment was proposed by Congress, February 6, 1869, and immediately sent to the
States for their ratification, and on May 4, the Ohio
Legislature forwarded to Congress a solution refusing to ratify the amendment, on the ground that Ohio
had, only two years before, by a large majority,
"rejected negro suffrage."* Though this action of
the General Assembly was not wholly unexpected,
yet it caused such a degree of excitement, and such
a significant pressure was brought to bear upon the
members of that body, that it convinced them that a
reconsideration of their resolution would not be un-
acceptable to the people. Moreover, it was plainly
evident that the amendment was going to secure
ratification by a sufficient number of States to insure
its becoming a law, regardless of the action of Ohio.
Consequently the Legislature wisely decided to
reconsider, and a motion for ratification was carried
in both houses, with only a meager majority in the
Senate. The vote stood 19 for, to 18 against.†
The joint resolution ratifying the amendment
received the signatures of the speaker of the
House and president of the Senate, January 27, 1870,
and was forwarded to Congress.‡ Two months later
it had received the ratification of the necessary number of States, and March 30 it was declared in force.
Universal male suffrage was henceforth the fixed

---

*Laws of Ohio, 66:424.

†Senate Journal, 66:44.

‡Senate Journal, 66:86.

policy of the United States. Ohio's reluctant ratification of the amendment had attracted the attention
of the whole country, and when she decided to follow the course which her sister States, some by incli-
nation, others by necessity, had adopted, a resolution
from both houses of our National Council was forwarded to Governor Hayes, congratulating "the
Legislature of the noble State of Ohio in her ratifica-
cation of the crowning measure of reconstruction."*
It is to be hoped that our Government will never
have cause to repent the course they then adopted,
and that the negroes in Ohio will never make themselves unworthy of the political privileges then
extended them. The passage of this amendment
ended the long struggle for political equality. Henceforth the negro in Ohio was to be legally the equal
in every respect of his white fellows.

---

*Senate Journal, 66:96.

CHAPTER III.

INFORMATION concerning the education of the colored people of Ohio is very limited. Previous to 1849 there was practically no State appropriation for colored schools. The few that were established were supported entirely by private subscription, largely by the colored people themselves, with an occasional help from their white sympathizers. Of these schools no systematic record was kept, and what knowledge of them we have been able to gain has been derived from fugitive pamphlets treating of the condition of the negro, anti-slavery tracts, and reports of anti-slavery societies and conventions. These schools were necessarily continued for only short terms, and at irregular intervals, even after 1849, when they were maintained by compulsory taxation the time seldom averaged over five months. They were usually held in the basement of some church or some abandoned old building—any place which could be secured for the least possible rent. Occasionally in a more prosperous negro settlement a small school-house would be erected and a teacher obtained, generally with the most indifferent qualifications, and who was paid the merest pittance. These teachers were generally a colored young man or woman, who, in spite of untold discouragement, had been able to acquire the rudiments of an educa-

tion, or some white person who was willing to work
for the little returns he might receive from one of
two motives, either because he could find no other
opening, or from a noble and unselfish purpose to
lift up the degraded and ignorant black children;
when this action meant only disgrace and social
ostracism, we cannot commend such self-sacrificing
teachers too highly.   With this preliminary account
of the early education of colored children in Ohio,
we shall now give a more connected and detailed
history of their educational opportunities, till the
time when all discriminations were abolished, and the
doors of our public schools were thrown open alike
to white and black.   The history divides itself naturally into two periods.   The first extends from the
formation of the State government in 1802 to the
repeal of the Black Laws in 1849.   The second, from
1849 till 1887, when colored children were received
into the public schools on the same conditions as
white children.

During the second period the law required the
establishment of separate schools in all districts containing a certain number of colored children, where
the authorities would not allow their attendance at
the regular white schools.   The Ordinance of 1787,
enjoined in Art. iii., that "Religion, morality and
knowledge being necessary to good government and
the happiness of mankind, schools and the means of
education shall forever be encouraged."   Thus, to
the honor of Ohio, be it said that the exclusion
of slavery, and the maintenance of free schools, were,
from the first, fundamental principles in our State
polity.   During the territorial stage of the State's
development, there were not over a few hundred

negroes north of the Ohio river, and it probably
never occurred to the framers of the ordinance, nor
to the early settlers in the Northwest Territory, that
the article above given could ever have the slightest
reference to the education of colored children in
Ohio. It is certain that no such interpretation was
ever placed upon the article by the law-makers of the
territory, nor of the State during the first forty-six
years of its history, as would entitle colored children
to a participation in the privileges of public schools.
The population in the territory was so scattered and
the resources of the government so limited, that
practically there was no public provision made for
schools at all. Liberal grants of land had been
made by Congress for the support of schools, and
the territory thought those would always be ade-
quate to sustain all the schools which should be
needed. This is apparent from Art. viii., Sec. 25,
of the Constitution adopted in 1802. During the
early years of free schools they were very unpopular,
and were looked upon as "charity schools." Of
course, it followed that a prejudice was created
against them, so that the idea of a public school
system was of very slow growth, the prevailing
opinion being for "every man to educate his own
children." Nearly twenty years passed before there
was any successful attempt made to establish free
public schools. Up to 1819 all legislative action
concerning them had been entirely of a local character. The Constitutional injunction to "encourage
schools and the means of education," had been
unheeded, but during this year (1819) a vigorous
effort was made in the General Assembly, by Ephraim
Cutler, to organize a school system, and a bill to that

effect passed the House, but was defeated in the Senate.* The following year a similar bill was introduced, and passed January 22, 1821, which laid the foundation for the public school system in Ohio. This law permitted the trustees of townships to levy a tax for the establishment of schools, but did not require it. The proceeds of the tax was to be used only in buying land, renting buildings and making up deficiencies in the education of poor children, whose parents were not able to pay tuition.† Although the modern idea of public schools does not seem to have been entertained by the members of the Legislature in 1821, yet the law was important as marking the beginning of our present school system. In 1825 a law was passed establishing a uniform system of taxation. The former law had left it to each district to determine its own taxation. By the new law county commissioners were directed to levy a half mill on the dollar, "to be appropriated for the use of common schools in their respective counties," and these schools were to be open "to the youth of every class and grade, without distinction."‡ Neither of these two laws made any mention of colored children, and although it was definitely stated that there should be "no distinction," it is not probable that the legislaors who framed and voted for it intended it should have such a signification. It is more likely that they never dreamed that such an interpretation would be given it, or that any one would think of admitting colored children to the white schools. There were not over 7,000 negroes

*Life of Ephraim Cutler, p. 113.
†Laws of Ohio, 19:5.
‡Laws of Ohio, 22:36; passed February 5, 1825.

in the whole State at that time and their presence
would not be seriously considered, and in some com-
munities where there might be only a few colored
children, their attendance would not be particularly
objectionable, but in most places the race prejudices
would generally be strong enough to shut them out,
even if by the law they were legally entitled to
admittance.   However, we find that whatever privileges they may have enjoyed in the schools were cut
off in 1829 by a law passed that year that "the
attendance of black or mulatto persons be specifically
prohibited, but all taxes assessed upon the property
of colored persons for school purposes should be
appropriated to their instruction and for no other
purpose."*   The prohibition was vigorously en-
forced, but the second clause was practically a dead
letter.   In some places no tax was assessed on colored
property owners, and in others, the money accruing
from that source was deliberately used for other purposes than for "instruction."   This same year (1829)
an act was passed to "incorporate and establish the
city of Cincinnati."   A similar provision was embodied in this act regarding the colored people in that city
as that in the earlier part of the year, thereby excluding the negro children from the city schools, and at
the same time making no provision whatever for
their "instruction" in any other manner.   As a
consequence they were left to shift for themselves,
receiving what aid they could from philanthropic
individuals and anti-slavery societies.   Of course the
great majority of free negroes who were attracted to
Ohio by her free Constitution settled largely in the
river towns.   It is said that fully one-third of their

* Passed February 10, 1829. Laws of Ohio, 27:72.

whole population was in Cincinnati alone, and here
we find the first effort to educate colored children
was made. As early as 1820 a few earnest colored
men, desiring to give their children the benefits of a
school, raised by subscription a small sum of money,
hired a teacher, rented a room, and opened a school;
but with such uncertain and limited funds it was possible to continue the school for only a few weeks,
and it was finally closed altogether. This experiment
was continued from time to time during the next ten
years in Cincinnati. In September, 1832, a small
Sunday-school was gathered, which in three years
numbered 125 scholars. In their zeal for improve-
ment, a lyceum also was organized, where three
times a week practical talks were given on different
literary and scientific subjects, and often an attendance of 300 would gather for instruction. A cir-
culating library of 100 volumes was also collected,
but owing to the inability of so many to read and
write, it was of little use, save for its value as an
inspiration. In March, 1832, an effort was again
made for a school. A suitable room was rented from
a colored man and a teacher secured. The room
was immediately so crowded that the teacher
found it necessary to resort to a rather unique scheme
to accommodate all who wished to attend. At 9
o'clock he called together about sixty of the smaller
children, and after they had all read and " spelled
around," dismissed them; when another division of
the larger ones took their places and went through
the same " curriculum." In the afternoon the same
arrangement was repeated, and in the same order.
The clamor of the adults to gain admittance became
so great that night schools were opened for two

evenings a week, the number of teachers necessary being obtained from Lane Theological Seminary from among the young men preparing for the ministry. This school soon assumed such proportions that three additional schools were demanded and organized, one exclusively for girls, where instruction in sewing was made especially prominent, and nothing was more needed, for the large majority of the girls were not only densely ignorant of letters, but still less the use of the needle and thread.*

The Lane Seminary students who had taken such an interest in mission work among the colored people formed no inconsiderable element in the seminary, and were thoroughly imbued with anti-slavery convictions. They " cast their lot" in with the interests of the "neglected mass of colored population," and established both Sabbath and day schools, and aided by a few philanthropic ladies in the city, accomplished much for their moral and intellectual elevation. But by the citizens and officers of the seminary their work was severely censured, and finally forbidden, and still further, all discussions upon slavery were expressly prohibited. As a result, in 1834, fifty-one

---

* I subjoin a composition by a scholar in the school, 16 years old, who had the opportunity of only a few months in school; it is really a very creditable production: " Let us look back and see the state in which the Britons and Saxons lived. They had no learning and had not a knowledge of letters. But now look at them. Some are now best men. Look at King Alfred, and see what a great man he was. At one time he did not know his a, b, c, but before his death he commanded armies and nations. He was never discouraged, but always looked forward and studied harder. I think if colored people study like King Alfred, they will soon do away with the evil of slavery. I can't see how the Americans call this a land of freedom where so much slavery is." Proceedings of Ohio Anti-Slavery Convention held at Putnam in 1835.

students withdrew from the seminary, and sustained a school for themselves till the following April, when they were induced to remove to Oberlin.* After their departure, the night schools, above referred to, were discontinued for lack of teachers. In Oberlin, under the nickname of "rebels," the seceding students were domiciled in a house roughly built of "slabs" to which the original bark still adhered. Their new quarters were dignified by the name of "Cincinnati Hall,"† and under this name became famous throughout the State. Anti-slavery principles were in no way incorporated in the original constitution of Oberlin College, and the question of admitting negroes into the institution was not even thought of by the founders, but the accession of these students from Lane brought the question to an issue. The trustees, in February, 1835, passed a resolution, carried, however, by only the casting vote of the presiding officer, to throw open the doors of the college to all students, irrespective of color. The "rebels" brought with them a young colored man, James Bradley, who had been a slave. He was the first colored student to enter Oberlin College, and consequently the first colored man to enter a collegiate institution in Ohio. From that time the number of colored students continually increased, and for many years previous to 1870 from four to five per centr of students in Oberlin College were colored.‡ The schools in Cincinnati continued to flourish, and the negro population in

---

*Pamphlet Statement of Reasons which induced the students of Lane Seminary to leave that institution.

†Oberlin, Its Origin, Progress and Results : An address prepared for the Alumni of the College, assembled August 22, 1860, by President J. H. Fairchild.

‡Address by President Fairchild referred to above.

the State increased till many other schools were established. Notwithstanding the discouraging circumstances which were met, we find that in 1838 there were colored schools and churches in the counties of Columbiana, Logan, Clark, Guernsey, Jefferson, Highland, Brown, Dark, Shelby, Green, Miami, Hamilton, Warren, Gallia, Ross and Muskingum. At the capital of the State there were two churches and two schools supported by the colored people. Of necessity the course of study in these schools was extremely limited, a knowledge of the three "R's" usually comprising the full course. But the zeal and sacrifice which they manifested to acquire even the simplest rudiments were truly wonderful, when we consider their past disadvantages and their present limited resources. The church and school generally stood side and side. The Methodist and Baptist churches were the leading denominations among the colored people. They had been the most active, as far as the law and the masters would allow, in missionary work among the slaves. The colored are as a class pronounced in their religious convictions, and the faith they accepted as slaves they retained as freemen. It is true that the moral standard of the negroes was not very high, and the depth and sincerity of their religion has often been questioned; but when we reflect that one-half of them had been slaves, when to lie and steal and deceive was wellnigh a necessity, to maintain even their very existence, when he was robbed of "his time, his wife, his children, and his very body and soul," it is not strange that the principles of morality did not develop a very high tone, nor that the habits formed under the con-

ditions of slavery should cling to him after he had
secured his freedom.

Regarding negro veracity, a young man who
taught in the " Negro Camps," as the colored settlements in Brown county were called, said, " Perhaps
the greatest fault of the colored men in the ' Camp '
is that they consider truth a shifty article. There
are many of them who do not stick at all times to
the truth and love it, even if it is ugly, but still there
is three times as much truth as we might expect to
find among beings placed in their circumstances."*
It is probably true that the disposition to " shift" the
truth was shared in, to a large extent, by the colored
people throughout the State, and in regard to the
other conventional fault of the negro—thieving—
the same latitude was too often allowed. The evidence, however, of the clerk of the Common Pleas
Court of Green county was to the contrary. The
colored population of this county in 1838 was 289,
yet out of this number, according to the sworn statement of the county clerk, " only four persons had
been convicted of crime in that county during the
preceding seven years ; of these, two were tried for
petit larceny, one for shooting with intent to kill, and
one for selling liquor without a license."† Three
citizens of Steubenville testified in the memorial to the
Legislature that the colored people in that place
"did not steal, or drink or quarrel more than the
white people."‡

Similar testimony could be multiplied from nearly

---

*Pamphlet—A Memorial of the Anti-Slavery Society to the
General Assembly, 1838.
†The Memorial above referred to.
‡The Memorial above referred to.

every county in the southern part of the State, but much of the evidence we now have respecting the moral character of the negro emanated either from their avowed friends and champions or from their enemies, and must not, therefore, be regarded as wholly unbiased. By this we would not be considered as implying that the friends of the colored people would purposely misrepresent the truth, but in their extreme sympathy for the oppressed race naturally they would incline to be "to their faults a little kind." On the other hand, the newspapers, dominated by Southern interests, and hence bitterly hostile to the negro, were ever ready to magnify every fault into a crime, and represented the free negroes in the State in the worst light possible.

It is difficult, in the midst of such partisan feeling and testimony, to draw a conclusion which will not be biased by the extreme sympathy of the one side or the extreme hostility of the other. This much, I think, can be soberly claimed, that considering their lack of an education, and their previous training, the colored people observed as high a moral standard as could be expected in their circumstances, and if there was a certain indifference to truth and honesty, it was not more conspicuous than among many whites who were in the same stage of economic and intellectual development. In any judgment we may pass upon the blacks in Ohio previous to the Civil War, caution should be used in our standard of comparisons; it would be unjust to apply the same that we would to the whites, who had never passed through the experiences and training which had made the colored what they were.

Coming back to the colored schools in the State.

In the northern section, the first of which I find any record was established in Cleveland in 1832, by John Malvin, who had formerly been a free colored preacher in Virginia, but had come to Cleveland in 1827, where he continued his work, doing odd jobs to pay his expenses.

Malvin had learned to read when a boy, in Virginia, and he at once tried to interest the few colored families in Cleveland to provide some means for the education of their children. A subscription guaranteeing $20 per month was raised for a teacher's salary, and the school was opened in 1832. Three years later, Malvin, who had proved himself an indefatigable worker, was instrumental in securing a convention at Columbus of the colored people of the State to devise some way of increasing the means to educate their people. The outcome of the convention was the organization of the School Fund Society, whose object was the establishment and maintenance of colored schools. Under the auspices of this society, schools were opened in Cincinnati, Columbus, Springfield and Cleveland, and were maintained for two years.*

In the southern section of the State the increasing colored population secured an increasing growth in the number and efficiency of the colored schools, which were supported largely by themselves, though the outside help was far greater in the cities than in country districts. In 1835, Cincinnati expended $1,000 in sustaining colored schools, of which the colored people gave $150, the rest being contributed by their friends. In 1839, the colored people paid

---

*J. H. Kennedy in Magazine of Western History, 12:130. Also Autobiography of John Malvin.

$889.03, and the self-sacrifice was not as great as in
1835, which showed a marked economic as well as
intellectual advancement. We must bear in mind
that few employments but day labor were open to
the colored people in the cities at that time, while
in the rural sections the men were mostly small
farmers, and as a consequence there was a greater
degree of independence and thrift. Wherever there
was a settlement of one hundred or more, there we
find a school for their children. In a small settlement in Gallia county a school of 25 scholars was
maintained by the colored people, who paid the
teacher $50 per quarter. In 1840 we find colored
schools in nearly all the large towns in the southern
part of the State. In some places the hostility of
the white portion of the place was so great that it
was impossible to have a school. Such was the case
in Jefferson, Scioto county, where in 1840 there were
one hundred negro farmers,* and most of them enter-
prising and prosperous, but the opposition was so
intense that no school was tolerated, and if any inter-
course was held between a white man and a negro,
he received the severest censure.† In several places
the whites burned the school-houses which the colored
had built, and sometimes their own private dwellings
were not safe from intrusion. Teaching a "nigger
school" was regarded as contemptible business, and

* Report on Condition of Colored People in Ohio, read by A. D.
Barber before the Anti-Slavery Society at Massillon, 1840.

†Report on Condition of Colored People in 1840, referred to
above. The extreme prejudice against the blacks is well illus-
trated by the following incident. A sister of Governor Lucas,
residing in Jefferson, employed a colored man on her farm; on that
account many of her white neighbors refused to associate with
her.

whoever engaged in it exposed himself to the scorn and sneers of his white neighbors, and was usually ostracised by white society. Nevertheless, the schools had "*come to stay*," and if one house was burned another was put up in its place, and teachers were not wanting who were willing to brave public opinion that they might help to lift up the oppressed and downtrodden. As years passed, the citizens of Ohio began to realize that the public welfare demanded the education of the increasing black population, and that the continuance of an ignorant, unprivileged class in the State was not only a positive disgrace, but might become a positive menace to the safety of the commonwealth. With this growing public sentiment was an equally growing desire on the part of the colored people for a more permanent and effective system for educating their children than by voluntary contributions. Although this subject had been repeatedly brought to the attention of the Legislature by petitions, and other ways, it was not till 1848 that any legislative action was secured. In February of this year an act was passed which provided that in any city or town where (*a*) twenty children were found who were desirous of attending school these shall constitute a school district, and the property of the colored residents shall be taxed for this purpose. The colored tax-payers were also authorized to elect their own directors from their own numbers, and these directors were to build and equip school-houses and have the entire charge of their management. (*b*) In any district where there were less than twenty colored children, and the property owners were taxed for school purposes, such children were to be admitted to the white schools, providing no written objection

be filed with the directors, signed by any person having a child in such school, or by any legal voter of
such district.   In case admittance was denied under
this proviso the tax collected from the colored for
school purposes was to be refunded.*

The utility of this law lay chiefly in the fact that
it was not left to the caprices of the colored people,
whether they should maintain a school or not, and
that the indifferent or negligent could be compelled
by law to pay for the support of a school wherever
there were twenty children who desired it.   The
burden was, therefore, more equalized by being
divided among the whole colored population of the
district, and thereby more permanent and efficient
schools were secured than those maintained by the
voluntary subscriptions.   The school law of 1848
marks a decided advance in the "ways and means"
of securing instruction to the colored people in
Ohio.   The object of the clause with reference to
the admission of colored children into the white
schools was probably to throw the responsibility
entirely upon the white people, and although it
granted the privilege to colored children, yet it was
under such conditions that in nearly every case it
would be denied, except in a few scattering districts
in the northern counties, where anti-slavery principles so predominated that there would be no objection to the intermingling of white and colored.   In
such cases the law would be a benefit to the colored
people.   This law, however, did not have the opportunity to determine its merits or defects, for it soon
gave place to the Repealing Act of 1849, which provided in regard to colored schools (a) that the trus-

* Passed February 24, 1848. Laws of Ohio, 46:81.

tees of each township, in case the colored were not
admitted to white schools, be authorized and required
to establish one or more school districts for colored
children. (*b*) The adult male colored tax-payers shall
assemble and elect school directors for such colored
schools. (*c*) All colored tax-payers shall be taxed
for schools of their own color, and for no other. The
special feature of this law was its absence of any
limitation of the number of colored children required
for the establishment of schools, and, barring the
initiative steps, left their complete supervision and
maintenance to the colored people themselves. The
first difficulty which arose under the provisions of this
law was that in many districts there were not more
than one-half dozen families of color, and the taxes
derived from them would be nothing more than a
mere pittance, and of course wholly inadequate
toward the support of a school long enough to
accomplish any good results, and unless the few colored children in the district could be permitted to
enter the white schools, they were deprived of any
school privileges.

Probably, on the whole, the law leaving the
schools to the supervision of the colored people themselves was the best plan that could have been adopted
at that time. Their management would certainly be
an education and an inspiration to them, notwithstanding their incapacity for their positive direction
(possibly not greater than the average white director) and the consequent detriment to the schools.
We find that generally the negro did not take kindly
to the establishment of separate schools ; they greatly
preferred admission to the white schools. At a convention of colored people held in Columbus a month

before the passage of the above laws (1849), it was resolved, "That the attempt to establish churches and schools for the benefit of colored persons *exclusively*, where they cannot enter upon equal terms with the whites, is in our humble opinion reprehensible."*

Notwithstanding the unwise eagerness to enter white schools, and the temptation offered to colored school directors to neglect their duties, in order to accomplish that object, yet the plan to leave the entire management of their schools to the colored people themselves until the time should come when they were equally eligible with the whites to an election of the regular boards, was no doubt the wisest and best plan.

Under this Act of 1849, many schools were established, but the statistics are so meagre regarding them that nothing very definite can be given, probably from the fact that not till 1853 were the reports of the State commissioners published. Cincinnati questioned the constitutionality of the act, and necessitated the colored trustees elected under the provision of the act to obtain an order from the Supreme Court of the State before they could draw from the city treasurer their quota of taxes, which came to them by a per capita division.

It appears that under the authority of the act, two colored school districts had been established in Cincinnati, called the Eastern and Western. School sessions were held in a church. Four teachers were employed, with an attendance of 845 colored children. The tax had been levied by a per capita division, white and black alike, and the amount due

*Minutes of the Convention of Colored Citizens of Ohio, convened at Columbus, January 13-15, 1849, p. 18.

the colored was $2,177.67. After a session of two months the colored trustees presented their bill to the city treasurer for that sum, that the payment of the teachers, rent and general expenses, might be made. The treasurer refused to pay the bill, on the ground that he had received no order from the city council to that effect. Obtaining no relief from the council, the trustees applied to the Supreme Court for a mandamus ordering payment. The court granted an alternative mandamus by virtue of which the council was instructed to order the payment of the bill, or appear before the court. The council preferred the latter alternative, and brought forward the plea that the act was unconstitutional, since it provided for the election of colored trustees, but a colored man could not constitutionally hold office in the State, and therefore there was no such body as the trustees of the Eastern and Western School Districts.

The trial was a spirited one, both sides putting forth every effort to secure judgment in its favor. The court decided that the office of school director, if it could be called an office, had never been recognized as such by the Constitution, and consequently it could not be unconstitutional for a colored man to hold it. The court therefore issued a peremptory mandamus directing the council to order the treasurer to pay the bills of the colored schools in like manner of white schools.* The colored people were of course highly elated over their victory, and applied themselves with increased earnestness and enthusiasm to the organization of their schools. We

---

* The State on Relation of Eastern and Western School Districts of Cincinnati vs. The City of Cincinnati, *et. al.* Ohio Reports 19:178 sq.

find that through all their discouragement the colored people never regarded the system of separate instruction as anything more than a makeshift, and accepted it because they could get nothing better. Their ambition was to enter the public schools on equal footing with the whites. The following year (1850) the revision of the Constitution offered them a favorable opportunity to present the subject, and a strenuous effort was made to secure a Constitutional guarantee of equal educational privileges.

The Committee on Education reported to the convention the following clause respecting the establishment of public schools: "The General Assembly shall make such provision by taxation or other means * * * * * as shall secure a thorough and efficient system of common schools free to all children in the State."

If this recommendation had been accepted, the colored people would have obtained their desire, but immediately upon the submitting of the report, a motion was made to insert "white" before "children," by Mr. Sawyer, the delegate from Auglaize county, who had before made himself conspicuous in the convention by his bitter hostility to the advancement of the colored residents of the State. The reason as given by Mr. Sawyer for his motion was that, aside from all social objections, the opening of public schools to the colored children would have a tendency to encourage negro immigration, and manumitted slaves and other free blacks would flock into Ohio from States where they were less favored, and thus Ohio would be burdened with the support of a still greater population of impoverished if not vicious negroes.*

On the other side, it was argued that while it might be politically inexpedient to enfranchise the negro, no such argument could hold against educating him, and if it was true, as represented, that the blacks formed an "impoverished and vicious" class in the State, it was high time they were offered every educational advantage which would enable them to earn an honest and reputable living. The vote on the motion was not recorded, but there is proof that it was carried.† The convention, however, wisely decided to omit all after the word "schools," and this left the settlement of all details about the management of schools to the Legislature, where it properly belonged. The report of the committee was accompanied by a minority report. This, while favoring all that was contained in the majority report, added a proviso to the effect that "black and mulatto youth should not attend the schools for white youth unless by *common consent*." ‡ This left the decision of the vexatious question entirely to the different districts. It is almost certain, however, that dispute must have arisen over the interpretation of the expression "common consent." It is assuredly ambiguous. Where there are two parties concerned, the natural interpretation would be the "common consent" of both parties. It is very obvious that the framers of the clause did not use it with such a sig-

* Debates of the Convention, 2:10.

† In speech made to strike out all the clause after "schools," Mr. Bates said: "I must express my regret and astonishment at the vote given a few minutes ago, by which the word 'white' was inserted." 3d Sec., Debates, 2:13.

‡ Debates. 2:18.

nification, much less did they mean the "common consent" of the colored people. We must therefore understand that only the "common consent" of *one* party to the transaction was intended. This application of the "Squatter Sovereignty" idea to educational matters must have found favor with many of the members, from the fact that a motion made to strike out the expression, and thus leave the proviso as definitely excluding the colored from all white schools, was defeated by a vote of 34 to 53.*

The convention was not yet ready to take final action on this very important matter, and therefore referred back to the committee the whole subject for reconsideration. It was not till a few weeks before adjournment that the convention took up the second report of the committee. The clause relating to the schools reported this time, was, after some revision of arrangement, adopted and ordered enrolled. It simply provided for the establishment and maintenance of an efficient system of common schools, which should always be free from any sectarian domination.† The question of who should participate in the privileges of the schools was left to the direction of the Legislature. Sawyer, determined to add one more stone to his memorial of injustice, intolerance and poor judgment, made a motion to amend, so as to secure the advantages of the schools to the white children only. It was, however, to the honor of the convention and the State, defeated.‡ The whole question was left to the Legislature to settle as circumstances and public sentiment might demand.

———

*Debates, 2:19.
† Constitution, 1850, Art. vi., Sec. 2.
‡ Debates, 2:699.

Though the revision of the Constitution did not result in opening the schools to the colored people, nor in materially increasing their educational facilities, yet the cause of negro education received that benefit which is always secured to any just cause by a free and full discussion of its merits. The colored schools continued under the operation of the old laws till 1853, when the General Assembly passed an act for the " reorganization and maintenance " of common schools.* The thirty-first section provided that school boards should establish one or more separate schools wherever the number of colored children in the district exceeded thirty. Whenever the attendance for one month was less than fifteen, the schools were to be discontinued, but the money paid by the colored was to be held and applied by the board for the education of the children as the board might judge best. Much to the dissatisfaction of the colored adults, the management of the schools was taken out of their hands and placed under the control of the regular school board. As might have been expected, they did not take kindly to the new arrangement, though it is now clear that such a change was really a step toward a single school system and the admission of colored into white schools.

In 1850 the Supreme Court of the State gave a very unexpected interpretation to the law of 1853. It decided, three of the five judges concurring, that the law was one of " classification" and not one of " exclusion ;" that the words " white" and " colored" as used by the act were used in their ordinary and popular signification, and that consequently children of three-eighths African blood and five-eighths white blood,

---

* Passed March 14, 1853. Laws of Ohio, 51:441.

whose complexion was distinctly colored, were not
by right entitled to admittance to the public schools.*
This decision was in direct contradiction to all previous decisions on this point.   The Supreme Court
had always maintained that persons having more than
one-half white blood should be entitled to all the
privileges of a white person.   The court had previously ruled that the " term white children in law described blood, not complexion," which would be an
unsafe guide.†   Again, in 1843, the court had decided that " youth of negro blood, but having more
than half white blood, should be entitled to the benefits
of the common schools."‡   Yet, contrary to all these
decisions, Judge Peck set aside every precedent and
followed the dictionary definition of a colored person,
rather than the legal one, which had been so repeatedly given by the Supreme Court.   We are obliged
to accept this action as another illustration of how the
courts were often completely under the dominion of
the slave-holding interest.   For a time it seemed as
if every sentiment of justice and humanity yielded
to the interests of the slave-owners in the South, and
to the prejudices of their sympathizers in the North.
As a consequence of this decision, not a few children
who possessed from one-fourth to one-eighth African
blood, and who had always been admitted to the
white schools, were now excluded, and though this
did not arouse as much resentment nor result in
as much mischief as it would have done ten years
before, yet the people of the State were justly indig-

---

*Van Camp vs. Board of Education of Logan County. Ohio
State Reports, 9:406.

†Williams ʋs. School District No. 6. Wright, Ohio Supreme
Court Report, p. 578.

‡Lane vs. Baker, Ohio Reports, 12:237.

nant at the high-handed way in which the judges had disregarded all precedent, and blushed that the State Supreme Court of Ohio had prostrated itself so low. In 1853, when the new law went into effect, there were in the State, according to the report of the State Commissioner, 6862 colored children of school age. But the school directors must have been very slow in organizing schools, as we find that only twenty-two schools were reported that year, with an enrollment of only 702 scholars, which makes only one-ninth of the whole number in the State, in school at all. In only twelve counties did the directors comply with the requirements of the law authorizing the establishment of schools. The superintendent of public schools in Columbus reported that a school had been organized there in accordance with the law, and seventy-five people enrolled, but for want of suitable rooms the school was discontinued till after the vacation. This may have been the case in many other places, and offers some explanation for the small number of schools in 1853. Cincinnati, under the law of this year, organized separate schools, and placed them under the management of the general board. Rightfully the colored people entered a vigorous protest against the change, for, under the law of 1849, they had been allowed to elect their own directors, who had full control of the schools, and they were very unwilling to give up this privilege, and be compelled to submit the management of their schools to white board of directors.

They claimed that inasmuch as they were alone taxed for the support of the schools, they should be allowed the supervision of them. It would seem that the whites were really jealous of granting the negro

any privilege which they could lawfully deny them.
But the colored people were so determined in their
opposition to the new system, that Cincinnati was
forced to compromise. A special act was therefore secured from the Legislature the next year, whereby the
colored schools in each district were placed under the
management of three colored directors, which should
be chosen, not by themselves, but by the regular city
board. These three directors should have full control of the schools, but were obliged to render to the
city board every month an account of their condition,
the funds expended, etc.* Though this act gave them
the direct management of the schools, it denied them
the election of their own directors, and the provision
requiring .monthly reports to the white board was
especially galling. They thought themselves capable
of supervising their own schools and controlling their
own finances, and continually chafed under the constant interference of the white people, but they made
no objection to reporting to the city council just as
often as the whites did, and in the same manner.
Their discontent finally became so great that the
whites were obliged to yield, and in 1856 a special
act was passed which provided that (a) the schools
in Cincinnati should be under the control of three
directors, who should be elected annually by the adult
colored citizens. (b) So much of the school funds
as would fall to the colored children by a per capita
distribution should constitute a school fund, subject to
the orders of the directors, and further, the directors
should annually send to the regular board an estimate
of the amount needed for school purposes, and this
estimate, either in whole or in part, as they should

* Passed April 18, 1854. Laws of Ohio, 52:48.

think best, should be included in their annual certificate to the city council, of the funds necessary to be raised for school purposes.* By virtue of this act the colored people of Cincinnati were made quite independent of the white board, except as they had the right to pass upon their estimate of school funds necessary for their schools.

The tax once levied and collected and the per capita division made, it constituted a school fund subject exclusively to the order of the colored directors The clause requiring a submission of their estimate to the regular board was thought necessary as a protective measure to the whites. Inasmuch as the negro paid but a small proportion of the taxes it was for their interest to make the estimate as high as possible.

This law placed the colored schools of Cincinnati on a substantial basis, and one satisfactory to the colored people. Their children had equal advantages with the whites ; only one desire remained ungratified, and that was admittance to the white schools, but for this they waited many years. This law which we have just described applied only to Cincinnati. In all other districts of the State the law of 1853, requiring the establishment of separate schools where colored children exceeded thirty, and placing them under the supervision of the regular board, was in force. In 1864 this law was so amended that the minimum number of children necessary for the establishment of schools was reduced from thirty to twenty, and the portion of school funds which would come to colored children by the per capita division was to be used exclusively for their educational purposes. The commissioner of

*Laws of Ohio, 58:417, passed April 8, 1856.

education gave instruction that when the number of children was less than twenty, the money due them for schools must be used each year in providing for them some means of an education. They might be admitted to the white schools if there was no objection made, and their share of the school fund should be used to pay their tuition. In some cases the white teachers organized evening classes for the benefit of such children, or a private teacher was sometimes hired, or, as it happened in many places, there was no provision made for them at all, and the taxes paid by them for the purpose was appropriated to other uses. The commissioner of education justly characterized such violation of the law as the "essence of meanness." While the per capita division was, no doubt, the most equitable that could be made, it was inadequate to provide suitable schools, from the fact that in most districts there were not enough scholars to support a school. In 1865 there were 626 districts in the State containing colored families. Of these only 171 reported over twenty children, and these so widely scattered that no one school could possibly accommodate all of them. The result was that unless they were allowed admission to white schools, they were practically denied all means of instruction.

The commissioner of education for 1865 said that it was his opinion that in about one-third of the districts where separate schools could not be maintained, the colored children were admitted to the white schools. Taking the State as a whole, the amount expended annually per capita for both whites and blacks was $3.50. The average wages in colored schools per week was $7.35. Hence a district con-

taining two colored children could maintain a school
for one week ; one of four could hold one two weeks,
and so on.   Even where there were twenty, they
could have only ten weeks in the year.*   In a State
which boasted of its free schools, such meagre provision for its colored children is astonishingly lamentable.   The same year (1865), the report of the
commissioner shows that in one district there had
been only $3.00 expended for the education of col-
ored children since 1853.   The commissioner cried
out against such rank injustice, and deeply lamented
the existence of a fastidiousness that would deprive
the colored youth of the State of *any* education,
rather than admit them to the white schools.   He
recommended that the law be so amended as to compel the authorities to continue the colored schools for
the same time as the whites, and that in case the
board of directors did not provide separate schools,
that the colored could demand their admittance to
white schools, and that their exclusion under such
circumstances be made a penal offence.†   This
recommendation was not followed, and it was many
years before such privileges were secured to the colored of the State.

The close of the Civil War had secured to them
equal rights with the whites.   The great political
boon for which they had contended for sixty years
was granted them.   They were at last citizens and
could deposit their votes as men.   Of course, race
prejudice still remained nearly as strong and unre-
lenting as ever.   The doors of white schools were
still locked and barred against them, but they had

---

* Report of State Commissioner of Education for 1865, p. 49.
† Report of the State Commissioner of Education for 1865, p. 49.

learned to "*labor and to wait*," assured that the time would come when they would be welcomed to the same halls of learning as their white brothers. By 1870 there were in the State only twenty-nine towns of over 500 population which reported colored schools, and none of these, with the exception of Fremont and Toledo, were in the northern counties. In all other northern towns they were admitted on equal terms to the white schools, and were generally treated with respect, though there was little disposition for the races to intermingle socially, or to fraternize with each other outside the school-room.

In the southern counties the prejudice, though waning, was still strong, and as late as 1871 a colored man in Norwich, Franklin county, applied to the courts for a mandamus to compel the school authorities to admit his three children to the public schools. His plea was that the law of 1864, authorizing a classification on the basis of color, contravened the Fourteenth Amendment, and was therefore unconstitutional. The court refused to sustain his plea, and ruled that colored children had no legal rights to claim admittance to white schools.* But the open door was inevitable. Many of the country districts in the southern counties, after 1870, no longer denied them admittance, and in the northern counties they were more and more pronounced in their readiness to welcome 'them. But not till 1887, twenty-two years after the close of the war, which granted them political independence, was it really secured.

---

* State of Ohio *ex rel*. William Garner vs. J. W. McCamm *et al*. 21 Ohio Stat., p. 198.

Through the efforts of Member-elect Arnett* and
James Turner, representative from Montgomery
county, a bill was introduced in the Legislature to
repeal all legislative action which denied the colored
children an equal participation with the whites in the
public schools. It passed the House without a dis-
senting vote. The law against intermarriage was
repealed at the same time.† This action of the
Legislature wiped out the last vestige of the "Black
Laws" from the statute books of Ohio. The day
(February 22, 1887) has always been regarded by
the colored people as a red letter day in their history.

We find that as a rule they have been eager to
improve their opportunities for acquiring an education, and the percentage of colored children in the public schools is probably as large as that of the whites, in
proportion to their numbers. The colleges throughout the State are open, and nearly every one has a
respectable contingent of colored students. I subjoin a table giving statistics regarding colored schools
from 1853 to 1869. Reports of them previous to
1853 are not available, as school commissioners' reports were not printed before that year.

———

* An educated colored man. He is now Bishop in African Methodist Episcopal Church.

† Laws of Ohio 84:34, and House Journal, 83:43.

A study of the table reveals some interesting facts. The most striking, perhaps, is the great difference between the number of colored youth of school age and the number enrolled in schools. In no year were there one-half; in some, not one-third, or even one-fourth in the schools. The average length of time in colored schools was about five weeks shorter than those of white schools, while the compensation per month was not materially different.

Closely akin to the intellectual condition of any people is their economic status. Indeed, the intellectual advancement is largely dependent upon economic circumstances, and on the other hand, to a great degree, education and good morals precede and promote a healthy and successful economic life. The pioneers of Ohio were a vigorous, keen-witted and sturdy class. The society which they established and developed was characterized by the same principles. The progress of the State was marvellous; older States looked in astonishment at the rapid growth in population and wealth attained by the new territory in the "free west." For much of her prosperity Ohio was largely indebted to the Ordinance of 1787.

The exclusion of slavery was the greatest blessing which could have been given her. It was no disgrace in Ohio to work; felling trees, grubbing stumps, splitting rails, preparing fields for cultivation was employment as honorable as any man could perform.

Pioneers from the East and sturdy emigrants from across the seas found in Ohio a home where the virgin soil was only waiting the opportunity to yield an abundant harvest, and where the owners thereof

could toil with their hands and still maintain their
social standing among their fellows. These inducements could not be offered in any of the slave States,
for free labor had no encouragement when work was
considered dishonorable. It was even maintained, and
with some truthfulness, that while slavery was a
curse to the South, it was a blessing to the Northern
free States, and its abolition would at least check their
rapid growth.

On this point, Caleb Atwater, who was one of the
earliest settlers in the Ohio Valley, and who has
contributed much to pioneer history, remarks, "The
growth and vigor and enterprise—the very blood of
the slave-holding States—now rolling into the Ohio
would be stayed, and turned back to other sources,
rendering those States not only more equal, but even
our superiors. Let slavery be continued one century
at least, and our descendants will go and settle in the
non-slave-holding States, as forest."* The above
statement may be somewhat highly colored, but the
main thought must be considered correct. The
younger sons from slave States, and home-seekers
from foreign shores were not slow in discerning the
prodigious strides Ohio was taking in education,
wealth and population ; in short, in everything which
goes to make up a progressive and prosperous commonwealth. The Southern States watched this
"speedy advancement" with no friendly interest, and
some of them were frank enough to admit the real
reason of it, and to acknowledge that unless a change
was made in their own policy, they would soon be
outstripped by the infant State of Ohio. The Richmond *Inquirer* in 1821 said : "It cannot be denied

*Atwater, History of Ohio, p. 331.

but that there is something in the policy of Virginia
which is unfavorable to speedy advancement in those
political and internal improvements which have ele-
vated some of the Northern States to a pitch of
enviable eminence, which but a few years ago were
our inferiors in rank, wealth and apparent prosperity,
and if the same causes continue to operate, the State
of Ohio, one of the youngest in the Union, and
formed out of the fragments of Virginia, bids fair to
rival the population of the Ancient Dominion itself.''*

In the same year a similar admission was heard
from Missouri, which had the year before been received into the Union as a slave State. The editor
of the St. Louis *Register*, regretting the course
which the State had taken, said : '' The result was,
as we predicted, those whom Missouri chiefly desired
to invite there will not come, because their property
can be much more profitably employed in the South ;
while the population which she *ought* to have desired, stops in Ohio, Indiana and Illinois, chiefly in
the former. The free laboring classes will not settle
in places where labor is considered degrading.''†
Such being the reputation of Ohio, it is not strange
that free negroes in the South, driven from their
homes by the tyrannical laws of the slave States,
should flock into Ohio.

When the State was admitted into the Union there
were but a few over three hundred negroes in the
territory, but during the decade from 1800 to 1810,
the negro population had increased more than five-
fold ; in the next decade it was nearly doubled, and
by the third it was fully so, so that in 1830 they

---

*Copied into Niles' Register of September 8, 1821. 21:28.

†Copied into Niles' Register of October 27, 1821. 21:132.

numbered over 9,500, making in round numbers one
negro to every ninety-five white men. This contingent was constantly increased by immigration of
free negroes, who, escaping the restriction imposed
upon them by the southern courts, hoped to better
their economic condition in a free State. In addi-
tion, occasional fugitive slaves found a resting-place
in Ohio, and remained, in spite of the constant fear
of being detected, captured and taken back to their
masters, or, what was worse, to be " sold down the
river." We find in the history of the early settlement of Ohio, that occasionally a kind-hearted slave-
owner, desirous of emancipating his slaves, and
knowing the disadvantages they would be under if
turned loose as " free niggers," would decide to
move into some free State, buy a tract of land and
settle his emancipated slaves upon it. Through all
these channels there was a continually increasing
negro population in the State. Very naturally, a
large proportion of the colored immigrants settled in
the southern counties along the river. Here the climate was more like that which they had been accustomed to, and in the loading and unloading of boats
there was always a demand for unskilled labor, and
by this work a great many negroes made a living by
means more congenial to them than the more continuous, if not more irksome, labor of farming. The
long intervals between their " jobs " gave them
ample opportunity to stretch themselves on some
plank, bask in the sun, and dream of the sweet
liberty they enjoyed. Of too many, it must be said,
they experienced more pleasure in dreaming than in
working, and as a consequence, they were generally
miserably poor, ignorant and too often wretchedly

vicious. But in this connection we must remember
that the conditions of life along any river are always
demoralizing, and the type of humanity which is
developed is usually of a like character, and hence
it would be unfair to consider the "dock negro" as
an average of his race in the State. On the contrary, we find that when opportunities were afforded
him to rise above the depressing influences which
always accompany extreme poverty, he showed himself proportionately industrious, hopeful and eager
to improve his economic condition.

But however ambitious and willing the colored
man might be to gain for himself by persevering
industry and integrity, a respectable livelihood, he
was always handicapped by the insurmountable prejudice against his race and color, by the constantly
recurring refusal of white workmen to be associated
with black ones, and by the law making it a penal
offence to hire a negro who could not present a certificate of freedom. * With all these hindrances in
his way, he found but few means of employment
available, which otherwise would have been open to
him. It was often quite impossible for a negro to
secure a certificate of freedom, and unless it was
generally acknowledged in the community that he
was legally free, many white sympathizers who were
really desirous of helping him were deterred from
giving him employment, lest they might be called to
an account by the courts. Notwithstanding, in com-
munities where the colored people had "half a
chance," they were generally industrious, and often
acquired considerable property. In 1835, there were
in Cincinnati, the centre of the colored population in

* Laws of Ohio, 3. p. 63.

Ohio, 2,500 colored people; of this number, 1195 had once been slaves, and had gained their freedom by purchase, manumission or escape; 476 had bought their freedom at an expense of $215,522.04, making the average price of each person $452.77. Some had earned their purchase money while still in slavery by working Sundays, cultivating a little patch of ground which had been allowed them by their masters, and by hoarding the small gifts which would from time to time be given the slaves. Sometimes an indulgent master would allow a favorite slave to buy his time; he would then hire himself out on a neighboring plantation, making some profit by the transaction. Others were permitted to go North, where they would have more opportunity to earn money, and here, by dint of hard work and most exacting economy, they would manage to collect the price of their liberty. In 1835 there were a large number in Cincinnati thus working out their freedom, the masters retaining their "free papers" for security. One woman paid for herself $400, and then earned enough to buy a little home valued at $600, every dollar earned by washing and ironing. The majority of freedom earners, as soon as their own was paid for, at once began to work for the freedom of a father, mother, brother or sister, who were still in slavery. Four-fifths of the colored people in that city had members of their families yet in bondage. Of course, it was only the kinder and more indulgent masters who would allow slaves to work out their freedom.

Many pathetic instances naturally occured in connection with the purchase of some beloved mother or other member of the household—I give only one example out of myriads of others like it. A young man who had succeeded in buying his own freedom saved $300 more, with the hope of buying his aged mother, whom he had left five years before in Virginia, that she might have the comfort of dying a free woman in a free State. Having heard she was for sale, he started immediately to purchase her. After traveling five hundred miles, he offered all his money for her, and—and—was refused. Not because he did not offer full value, nor because she was not for sale, but—she had four sons and daughters together with her whom the owner thought would sell to greater advantage by keeping the family together and selling them down the river. The loving, stricken son pleaded in vain for his mother, but the owner was inexorable. He would not sell and the poor boy returned with a heavy heart to Cincinnati. He learned afterwards that the whole family were sold in New Orleans.* The free negroes in Ohio at that time who had bought their own freedom and perhaps that of others of the family, were above the general average of colored people. They had usually been house servants and favorites with their master or mistress, and were of the more intelligent and industrious class. Some of them showed quite decided ability, and were able to make themselves comfortable and independent.† But they

---

*Report on the Condition of the Colored People, read before the Ohio Anti-Slavery Convention held at Putnam, April 22-24. 1835. From the same source I have derived my other statistics regarding the colored people in Ohio.

†Rebecca Madison paid $1,000 for freedom, and then earned for herself $3,000.

Henry Boyd bought himself at the age of 18. By the time he was 31 he was worth $3,000, and had bought brother and sister for whom he paid $900.

had to fight against fearful odds; race prejudice
shut them out of all the more lucrative occupations,
and limited them to the more menial forms of daily
labor. The heads of families were generally common laborers, cooks, waiters or washerwomen,
while the children picked up jobs on the street, run
on errands, cleaned walks, blacked boots, and sold
newspapers, did anything to earn a penny. Occasionally a mechanic would be found, but the difficulty
of finding employment generally discouraged them
from trying to learn a trade. A few, especially
thrifty and ambitious, would go into business for
themselves. According to Williams, the first fancy
grocery store in Cincinnati was established by a
colored man, while another, according to the same
authority, invented and manufactured the "Boyd bed-
stead," which for a time had considerable sale, but
the inventor, being a colored man, was debarred
from taking out a patent, and it was secured by a
white man.*

In the rural districts their condition was better than
in the cities, for here they could own small farms,
and they managed them with a good degree of skill,
for while slaves they had been accustomed to farm
labor and were, therefore, better prepared to do that
work than any other. Nearly all the southern counties had one or more colored settlements. In Pike
county, 1840, there were 33 colored families, which
together owned 2,225 acres of land. In Shelby
county there were 265 colored inhabitants, who
owned 4,286 acres well stocked with horses, cattle
and sheep. In Dark county, 281 persons, who
owned between four and five thousand acres. In the

---

*Williams' History of the Negro in America, 2:194.

town of Lancaster there were 20 individuals who owned real estate valued at $17,000. In Columbus there were in 1837, 23 colored men who were owners of property to the same amount ($17,000). A colored man in Cincinnati, who was a slave till he was 24 years of ago, acquired two houses and lots valued at $10,000, besides owning 320 acres of land in Indiana; in 1840 his property was valued between twelve and fifteen thousand dollars.* While these figures are sufficient to show that some of the colored people were endowed with no mean ability, and could by faithful industry secure for themselves and their families a respectable livelihood, yet they rather indicate what was possible than what was the actual average condition of them, for the majority of them were poor and too often indolent, and it was a hard struggle for a living, but inasmuch as their standard of living was not very high, they were satisfied with a degree of comfort which would have been intolerable to their white neighbors, in the same circumstances.

The success of the few was often used as capital by the friends of the negro to refute the claim that a free negro could not provide for himself. On the other hand, where they had shown themselves strikingly inefficient, and incapable of earning a comfortable living, their enemies would flaunt such instances as conclusive proof of the inferiority of the negro, and as sufficient justification for slavery. For many years the really disreputable condition of the colored settlements in Brown county was used as a

*These figures are taken from the Report of Condition of Colored People in Ohio, read before the Anti-Slavery Society, May 27, 1840, by A. D. Barber.

stock argument by slave owners, among Northern
sympathizers, against the usefulness of the abolition
of slavery. It seems that in 1820 about one thousand
colored people, mostly emancipated slaves, had settled in Brown county, on land purchased for them.
They had the free use of the land, but could not sell
it. It was expected they would be industrious enough
to earn a decent living, if nothing more. The result
was that the "Camps," as these settlements were
called, became notorious for their wretchedly shift-
less condition, and for the immorality of their inhabitants. The Cincinnati *Gazette* in 1835, fifteen years
after their establishment, pronounced the following
judgment upon them :   "They are so extremely lazy
and stupid that the neighboring farmers will not
employ them to any extent. They do not raise produce enough on their own lands to keep their families,
much less do they have a surplus to sell abroad.
They pass most of their time in little smoking cabins,
too listless to even fiddle and dance. One may pass
through the 'negro camps,' passing a dozen strag-
gling cabins, with smoke issuing out of the ends
of them, in the middle, little clearings, without seeing
a soul, either at work or play. The fear of starva-
tion makes them work the least possible quantity,
while they are a great deal too lazy to play. There
are not more than two or three families out of the
whole who have been benefited by the change from
slavery to freedom."* This judgment is obviously
not free from prejudices and partisanship, and their
condition, bad enough at the best, is no doubt somewhat exaggerated. The most generous of the negro

*From *Cincinnati Gazette*, copied into Niles' Register of October
3, 1835, vol. 49, p. 76.

friends considered the experiment as unsatisfactory.* Working under the lash, at the order of an overseer, was quite a different matter from working as one's own master. Slavery, while it accustomed its victims to toil, did not train them to independent and thrifty habits of industry, hence, why should it be considered a "strange thing under the sun" that when emancipated and suddenly transplanted to the North, settled on a piece of land and left to shift for themselves, their sudden liberty made them indolent, careless and improvident. The settlement in Brown county shows the negro in Ohio, in his worse condition, while those of Pike and Shelby counties exhibit him probably at his best; the majority of them were between the two extremes.

At no time did they take kindly to any scheme to colonize them, either on the coasts of Africa, or on the shores of the North Pacific. The plan for negro colonization, which was proposed November 6, 1816, at Princeton, New Jersey,† was fully developed the following year and as a result, The American Colonization Society was organized, with James Madison as president. A branch society was soon after organized in Ohio, but the free negroes here, as in other States, made war against it.‡ By them the plan was regarded as only a scheme to perpetuate slavery, and that their colonization was simply to remove from the South the population of free negroes, whose freedom was thought to be a continual cause of discontent and

---

*Barber's Report, referred to above.
†Niles' Register, December 14, 1816. Vol. 11, p. 260.
‡Resolutions condemning Colonization passed by colored people of Philadelphia. Niles' Register, 17:201, and by Convention of Colored People of Ohio held at Columbus, 1879.

insurrection among the slaves; they were, therefore, naturally opposed to it. The advocates of
colonization, not proposing to interfere with the
slaves in the South, believed that the removal of the
free negro population would eventually secure the
emancipation of all slaves. Beyond question, the
greater part of the Colonizationists were sincerely
desirous of improving the condition of the free
negroes, and thought it a peaceful way for the future
termination of the great evil of slavery.

The project gained adherents very rapidly, and
soon became immensely popular throughout Ohio
and the North. Every way was tried to interest the
colored people—tracts were distributed, lectures and
sermons were delivered, and conventions were
held, and yet a comparatively few converts were
secured, the approval of the majority of the
colored people was never gained, and no great
number was ever induced to emigrate to the
colony. To encourage emigration of all who
were willing but were prevented by lack of means,
philanthropic persons offered to pay the transportation of a certain number. In 1831, James Perry and
R. Wallace advertised in Cincinnati to "feed, clothe
and pay the transportation of 15 able-bodied men for
one year's faithful service from each man."* But
they were determined to stay in Ohio, and "fight it
out along the old line," rather than to "fly to ills
they knew not of."

There were others who advocated colonization
from entirely different motives than those of benevo-
lence or love for the negro, because they wanted to
get rid of them, and so be relieved from any respon-
_____
*Reprinted in African Repository, August, 1831.

sibility to improve their moral and social condition. These latter were quite as active and zealous as the former, and while generally working in harmony, were animated by entirely different motives. Petitions were presented to the Legislature, praying for aid, and the attention of the Constitutional Convention of 1850 was called to the subject. Here the question of State appropriation became a sectional one. The members from the southern counties, where the negro population was the largest, generally favored the project, while in the northern ones, where there were but few colored people, and anti-slavery feeling was strong, it received but little support.* Some opposed it on the ground of injustice and humanity, others, especially northern members, because the whole State would be taxed for the benefit of the southern counties. It was argued that State aid for colonization, without at the same time prohibiting immigration to the State, would place a premium on immigration and the negroes would flock into Ohio in order to secure transportation to Africa, thus making Ohio a general thoroughfare for all negroes immigrating to the colony; or, to quote the forcible language of one of the members, "Ohio would become a great lazar house for all runaway and emancipated negroes around us."

Those who argued along this line, either from ignorance or intention, entirely misjudged the temper of the negro, but few of them, as we have said before, wanted to emigrate, and vigorously opposed all efforts made to induce them to do so. They maintained that inasmuch as the whites had brought them to the United States, here they were going to stay,

*Debates of Convention, 2:604.

and the whites must suffer the consequences of their own folly and wickedness. The decided creditable attitude of the negroes toward the colonization scheme was no doubt due in a great measure to the few of their number who by superior ability and education were able to exercise a controlling influence over them. I do not think I exaggerate in saying that a few colored leaders practically determined the policy of all the rest, from the fact that the better informed and more industrious were as a rule contented to stay where they were. By their example and influence they were continually stimulating their fellows to the cultivation of habits of industry, frugality and providence; such habits the negroes as a class have always been slow to learn.

The advent of the Civil War greatly affected the economic condition of the colored people, by lessening the extreme race prejudice, by opening up new fields of employment, by softening the bitter antipathy which white workmen felt against laboring with them, and by the development of a better fraternal spirit among all classes. These results have been the means of greatly eradicating hatred and intolerance toward them, and giving them a more equal chance with white men in the struggle for a livelihood. The systems of trades unions and labor organizations, which occupy such a prominent place in the industrial life of our country at the present day, have largely been created since the Civil War. Previous to that time there were organizations of moulders, cigar-makers and printers, and constitutionally the negro was not excluded; but the members always reserved the right to reject any applicant, whether white or black, and as a fact, it was seldom,

if ever, that a colored man could be found, before
1865, who was a member of any labor association.
The Knights of Labor, which date from 1869, and
the American Federation of Labor, organized in
1880, make no distinctions, nor requirements for
membership, on account of color. It is, however,
left to the local societies to accept or reject any applicant they wish, and as a result, in sections where
race prejudice is strong, the negro is excluded ; but
where it is weaker, a colored applicant is occasionally
admitted, but it is rare that we find in any labor association more than a small membership of colored
men.

The leaders of these societies do not admit that
this is due to any discriminations on their part, but
that the fault lies entirely with the negroes themselves,
because of their unwillingness to enter any regular
trade. On the other hand, some prominent colored
men in the State make an entirely opposite claim,
and maintain that they are limited to menial labor
because they are excluded from labor unions. The
truth doubtless lies between the two extremes, that
while there is no constitutional objection, in many
local societies the "color line" would still be an insurmountable objection, for them to secure membership. The truth remains that not many negroes
incline to mechanical pursuits which demand close
and persistent application. It is not an easy matter
to eradicate the effects of compulsory labor, and
that of the simplest form, so that they can ever embrace the perplexing and complicated methods of
preparation for a trade necessary to enable them to
stand on lines of equality with those who have never
known the demoralizing effects of such experiences.

While labor federations may, and probably do sometimes debar really ambitious and industrious colored
men from obtaining the employment they could wish,
yet others may make it an unwarrantable stock excuse
for not preparing themselves for the various depart-
ments of skilled labor, to whose open doors are
equally invited all classes of earnest, industrious
men, be they white or black.

CHAPTER IV.

OBSERVATIONS UPON THE SLAVERY SENTIMENT IN OHIO.

THE history of public sentiment in Ohio regarding slavery is somewhat different from its history in the older States in the Union. In all the "original thirteen" and in every other State till the admission of Ohio, slavery was at some time legally sanctioned, and was not opposed by the moral sentiment of the people. In the northern colonies the opinion regarding it soon began to change, partly owing to the strong religious influence of the Puritans and Quakers, who felt that human bondage was wrong, and contrary to every principle of truth and righteousness. Another influence among them was economic. Slavery was not profitable in the North; neither the climate nor the soil was adapted to secure the best results from negro labors; "it did not pay," and, therefore, it could never secure a strong foothold there. Whenever it was allowed for a time, the time was short, and soon disappeared altogether. While the principle of self-interest rather than moral conviction may have dominated the sentiment and legislation regarding slavery in the Northern States, yet it was the iniquity of the system which appealed to the people with the greatest force, and ultimately produced that uncompromising hatred of human bondage which would not be satisfied till slavery was forever

banished from the country. Public opinion, regarding the right or wrong of the question, if not at first
fully settled, we find at length rapidly assuming the
position which it has ever since unquestionably maintained, and by the time Ohio was opened up for settlement, the advocates and opponents of the system
were lined up for battle which was destined to rage
till the last vestige of negro bondage was swept from
the land.

By 1802 the South had taught themselves not only
to believe in the profitableness, but the righteousness
of their "peculiar institution," and were strongly
fortifying their position on both moral and economic
grounds. In the North, while not yet disposed to
interfere with slavery where it already existed, still
there was a pronounced opposition to its extension,
and an ever-increasing desire to see its complete extermination.

Ohio, therefore, never witnessed the earlier
phases of anti-slavery sentiment. The early settlers
from the Eastern States who came into the Northwest
Territory had their convictions firmly established on
the question of slavery, and of restricting it to its
then present boundaries, and that the new lands
should be forever consecrated to freedom, and were
ready to defend their principles against any attempt
to fasten the evil system upon their adopted country.
From the South there came no small emigration, who
would gladly have brought their slaves with them,
and could see no reason why they should be deprived
of their "home comforts" by coming to Ohio. Notwithstanding, there was always sufficient anti-slavery
sentiment to command a decided vote against its admission to the State, consequently Ohio, unlike In-

diana, never made any protracted effort to secure a
suspension of the non-slavery clause in the Ordinance
of 1787. I think we can gain a better understanding
of the feeling in Ohio respecting the question of
slavery by classifying the people according to their
convictions, into five distinct groups, which could be
found in the State between 1802 and 1865.

1. There was a small but determined party of pro-
slavery men. These were mainly from the South,
who had been attracted to the new State by the health-
fulness of its climate and the fertility of its soil, who
deemed slave labor indispensable for opening up a
new country, and really thought that its introduction,
for a limited period at least, would be of incalculable
benefit to the growth of the State, and they could not
possibly see any moral or economic objection to
bringing their slaves with them. Failing in their
efforts to transplant their " peculiar institution," they
generally became discontented and dissatisfied, and
aided by their brethren across the river, were often
leaders in the disgraceful and inhuman attacks upon
the free negroes and their white sympathizers. This
class was sometimes recruited by emigrants from the
Eastern States, who were naturally opposed to slavery,
but settling along the Ohio river, were in close
proximity to slave territory, and soon established social and business relations with the slave-owners across
the river. Attracted at first by the royal grandeur of
a southern plantation, and charmed by the sumptuous
hospitality of its master, they soon envied his lordly
position, and would gladly have created a like one
for themselves, thus becoming blind to the evils of
slavery, they soon became enthusiastic sympathizers
with the southern interests, like vice when

" Seen too oft, familiar with her face,
  We first endure, then pity, then embrace."

2. The second group included those who had no
moral scruples against slavery, and did not object to
its indefinite extension, provided it did not reach over
into their own State. They believed slavery in the
South to be a blessing to the North, inasmuch as the
more desirable immigrants would settle in those States
where work was honorable, and as a consequence the
prosperity of the North would thereby be secured,
partly at the expense of the South. These were
governed by the principle that " self-love was the
instrument of their preservation."

3. The third class looked upon slavery as an evil,
but a necessary one, and did not believe that its extermination was possible. They would restrict it to
its present boundaries if it could be done without
antagonizing too strongly southern interests. They
would allow new States the greatest latitude in deciding whether they should be " free " or " slave." To
them slavery was only a system of labor, an expen-
sive one, they admitted, to the employer and unjust
to the laborer, but for the slave as an individual they
had no special sympathy ; they regarded him simply
as a representative of an unfortunate race. Neither
did they have any disposition to grant to the free
negro the privileges which a free man could
reasonably expect in a free country, and in his
struggle to earn an honest livelihood against all the
disadvantages of race prejudice and hatred, they
had no compassion nor assistance to render. To
this class southern slave-owners always looked, and
generally found help in recapturing their runaway
slaves. It was probably the largest and most influen-

tial class in the State. They dominated politics, made the laws, filled the offices, and sat upon the judicial bench. They were mainly responsible for the infamous " Black Laws," which disgraced the statute books of Ohio till 1849.

4. This group believed that slavery was morally and economically wrong. They would not only prohibit its extension, but in every way possible lessen the evils of its operation where it already existed. They made a "virtue of necessity" and endured it, simply because they judged its extermination a thing impossible. They looked upon the whole system as the Nation's skeleton in the closet, and believed that the "better part of valor" was to avoid discussion lest someone's "feelings" would be hurt, and they were willing to wait "the fullness of time" when it would be expedient and safe to agitate the question. To this class belonged the large body of Colonizationists, who verily thought that the abolition of slavery was only a "question of time." They were for the most part zealous, sincere and really philanthropic people, but they never truly grasped the slavery problem and were wholly mistaken in their means for its solution.

5. This fifth class constituted those who in the popular phraseology of the day were called the "pronounced anti-slavery people" or the hated "Abolitionists." They believed in, and worked for, the immediate abolishment of slavery in all the States in the Union. To them it was never a question of expediency or forbearance, it was simply a principle of right and wrong ; they admitted no Constitutional right to human property. They formed the "bone and sinew" of all anti-slavery effort. They brought

their sentiments "to the front" by a continuous
round of lectures, tracts, newspapers and private
conversations, keeping an increasing agitation of the
question before the public mind.

They opposed the colonization scheme, on the
ground that there was but one solution of the problem,
and that a whole and entire abolition of the institution
of slavery. This class was always a friend and
helper, not only to the free negroes, but to the fugitive in his flight toward freedom ; they were always
ready to give rest and protection. It was against
this class that the southern slave-holders hurled their
most stinging anathemas—they considered no epithet
too vile or too severe to be heaped upon them. While
this class believed in abolition, they differed somewhat
in their ideas of the best means of obtaining the end.
These differences may conveniently be considered
under three heads. (a) Those who held that the
Constitution was a "compact with hell" and considered any acceptance of the voting privilege as absolutely wrong. These were the Extremists, and were
the followers of William Lloyd Garrison. Their
number was never very large in Ohio, and they exerted no special influence in the State politics. While
they were sincere and honest in their convictions,
yet their extremely radical and uncompromising
attitude unfitted them for a practical co-operation
with the rest of the Abolition party.

(b) Those who, cutting loose from the old parties, thought it best to organize a third party, known
as the Liberty party. Among its most efficient members were Edward Wade, Leicester King, Robert
Morris, and after 1840, Salmon P. Chase, though he
continued to act on most questions with the Demo-

cratic party, and in 1849 was sent by it to the United States Senate. James G. Birney was, perhaps, the most prominent member of the Liberty party. He was Presidential nominee in 1840 and again in 1844. It finally merged into the Free Soil party, which in 1849 held the balance of power in the State legislature, and secured the repeal of the odious "Black Laws."

(c) The third division included all who were strongly anti-slavery in their convictions, but continued in their old parties. The anti-slavery Whigs urgently protested that their party must adopt the Constitutional anti-slavery ground, while the Democrats as vigorously protested the same respecting their party, but neither desiring to sever their connection with the old party. Among the foremost in their zeal against slavery, but still adhering to their old party, were Joshua R. Giddings and B. F. Wade. Between the (3) and (4) groups, mentioned before, there was a constant clashing; the Colonizationists regarded the Abolitionists as visionary fanatics, attempting the impossible, and in a way strikingly objectionable to the southern slave-owners. The Abolitionists rejoined by claiming that the Colonizationists were attempting to rid themselves of responsibility by shipping the negroes to Africa, and that the idea of a gradual emancipation was nothing less than a compromise with evil. The two often came into violent collision, and in their eagerness to see the success of their own pet means, allowed their rivalries and jealousies so far to govern them as really to lose sight of the end in view. The following incident will illustrate the bitterness of feeling which sometimes existed between them. A joint debate was

held in Cincinnati, March 4–5, 1839, on the question, " Is the American Colonization Society worthy
of the confidence and charities of the American people ? " The affirmative was supported by Rev. R.
R. Gurley, of Washington, D. C., an agent of the
Colonization society. The negative was maintained
by Rev. J. B. Blanchard, pastor of the Sixth Presbyterian Church, of Cincinnati. A local paper,* favoring colonization, gave the following account of the
first day's proceedings : " Mr. B. Blanchard, as the
challenging party, commenced his argument. His
remarks were made up of the slang and bombast
which has characterized the abolition papers and lecturers from time immemorial. We have never seen
a man so completely used up, or false reasoning so
fully exhibited in its true light, as by Mr. Gurley's
replies. The rotten fabric upraised by the Abolitionist was demolished in an instant, his rather sophistical
declaration was shown up in its marked deformity."
It is obvious from this report that partisan spite and
extravagant language is not original with modern
reporters. The churches, as a rule, during the first
forty years of anti-slavery struggle in the State, were
more in sympathy with the aims and methods of the
Colonization society than with the Abolitionists. In
Cincinnati, 1837, there was not a single white church
which would open its doors for a discussion of the
principles of the Abolitionists.† The Methodist
Church, which later was in the vanguard in the battle against slavery, at its conference in Springfield,

---

* African Repository, xv., p. 112, citing Cincinnati Republican
for March 5, 1839.

† Report of Anti-Slavery society, convened at Mt. Pleasant,
Ohio, April 27, 1837, p. 26.

1835, passed resolutions heartily commending the objects of the Colonization society, and declared itself fully in accord with its "aims and methods," and at the same time condemned in unequivocal terms the course pursued by the Abolitionists, and called upon "its preachers, local brethren and private members to abstain from any connection with them."*

The next year, at the general conference held in Cincinnati, two members were severely censured for speaking in favor of abolition. A resolution was passed disclaiming any "intention or wish to interfere with the civil and political relation between the master and the slave, as it exists in the slaveholding States in this Union." But the members were not unanimous on the resolution, and a protest was entered, signedby the New Hampshire and New England delegates.

The breach between the North and the South was rapidly widening, which would and did split the Church in twain. The Presbyterians were even more conservative than the Methodists. During all the early years of the anti-slavery agitation, they discountenanced abolition and urged a *laissez faire* attitude, but personally favored colonization, and the outcome of their position was, North and South Presbyterian churches, and General Assemblies, North and South. This classification of the public sentiment of Ohio, which has been given, must not be understood as holding good in every instance, for no hard and fast line can be drawn between the different groups ; they generally so merged into each other that we find some Abolitionists who favored colonization as an expedient for improving the condition oi

* African Repository, November, 1835, p. 332.

the free negroes, and *vice versa*, there were firm
champions of colonization, who hoped and prayed
for abolition, and there were those out-and-out pro-
slavery in their convictions, who supported colonization by their money and their votes, some, to rid
themselves of troublesome "free niggers," others
from a true regard for their welfare.

Our study has not only to do with the opinions entertained by the people of Ohio regarding slavery,
but also with the various ways in which these opinions
found expression.   Ohio has ever been characterized
by its activity and fearlessness. The people have
always been ready to sustain opinion by action. The
deed has closely followed the word. This was equally
true in their manifestation of opinion regarding slavery.   The pro-slavery sentiment found its expression
in at least four different ways, first, in a general
prejudice against the free negro, by those who so
fully believed in negro slavery as to desire its establishment in Ohio ; by those who were unwilling to
interfere with it, however much they were opposed to it
in principle ; and by those whose social and business
interests were so intimately connected with it that they
were ranked among the enemies of the free negro.
This class in Ohio was a constant source of annoy-
ance and irritation to the slave-owners.   Their freedom excited the envy of their fellows in bondage,
and made them discontented with their situation, and
as a consequence a slave insurrection was constantly
feared.   To counteract this influence the most cruel
laws were passed restricting the rights of the free
negro, depriving them of social and legal privileges,
and in some States going so far as to eject them from
the State.   With such a prevailing sentiment it was

quite natural that Northern sympathizers with slave-owners should be more or less impressed by it. Even the majority of Abolitionists themselves never thought for one moment of meeting them on a plane of social equality, although some professedly acknowledged them as their equals. But they were the exceptions which prove the rule.

Many churches in the southern counties virtually closed their doors against them, or if admitted, they were usually restricted to a place in the gallery, or in some obscure corner. As late as 1849, the colored people in convention in Columbus protested against the unchristian discrimination of the "negro pew." With such a precedent from the churches, one is not surprised at their exclusion from the public schools. This same feeling was shown in hotels and restaurants. The proprietors served their patrons with colored servants, but on no account would entertain a colored man. Railroads and stage coaches placed them at great inconvenience, and their officials often subjected colored passengers to positive insults. Theatres and other public places of amusement followed the same line of treatment, and either closed their doors against them altogether, or restricted them to some undesirable part of the house. The expression, "nigger heaven," meaning the upper gallery of a theatre, which is yet common, no doubt had its origin in these early restrictions on the colored people. In Cincinnati there was a theatre with the inscription over the door, "Niggers and dogs not admitted." To say, that many times, and in many places, and by many men, they were not treated much better than dogs, would not be putting the case too strongly.

We have before indicated how limited were the fields in which a negro could find employment; how sympathy with southern interests, or race prejudice, blocked every avenue to his moral, intellectual and economic advancement; how he was handicapped at every turn, and persecuted on every side. I ask, is it not marvelous that he did as well as he did ?

This hostility of the whites did not limit itself to unjust laws and social discriminations, but found vent in armed attacks upon the negroes and their white sympathizers. One of the most cruel and atrocious of these assaults was perpetrated by the white people of Cincinnati in 1829, an account of which has already been given in a preceding chapter. Unpardonable as they were, we find that they were often winked at by the authorities, and the perpetrators seldom punished, and as it sometimes happened, the civil and police officers joined in and encouraged the mob in its lawless invasion of human rights. As one of the most notorious of these mobs, we would cite the one of 1836, when J. G. Birney was the prominent victim. He was a native of Kentucky, and the son of a slave-owner, but being thrown under anti-slavery influences, he early imbibed an intense hatred of the whole system. Growing to manhood, he found himself practically ostracised in his native State on account of his anti-slavery principles. He resolved to move to Ohio, and took up his residence in Cincinnati. He soon became satisfied that he would serve the cause best through the publication of a paper devoted to the principles of abolition. When his intentions were rumored in the city, the papers denounced him and his cause in the most unequivocal terms. The Cincinnati *Whig* said of his enterprise : "We deem this new effort a new insult to our slaveholding neighbors, and an attempt to brow-beat the public in this question."* Mr. Birney having assured himself that he could have no guarantee of protection from the city authorities, deemed it prudent to publish his paper outside the city jurisdiction, and accordingly established himself at New Richmond, a small village a few miles up the river, and on January 11, 1836, issued his first number of the *Philanthropist*. The name was the same as that of a paper published in 1817–1818, at Mt. Pleasant, by a Quaker, Charles Osborne.

The issue was eagerly awaited, Mr. Birney's enemies hoping to find something by which they might excite the popular passions against him and his friends. But in this they were disappointed. It was remarkably moderate, and free from anything which might arouse the hatred of his opponents.

The leading article claimed the absolute necessity for such a paper—that the preservation of liberty of speech and of the press demanded it. "The truth is," said the writer, "liberty and slavery cannot both live in juxtaposition."† The history of the final overthrow of slavery has fully vindicated the truth of his statement. The monster was not contented to dominate in the South—it could not be satisfied till it had extended its octopodan claws across the border, and stifled free speech and a free press in the free States. The Whigs and Democrats alike joined hands in assailing Birney and his paper

——

* Birney's Life of Birney, p. 209, citing the Cincinnati *Whig* of December 21, 1836.

† Birney's Life of Birney, p. 210.

in the most abusive language.   Before the paper had
reached its fourth issue, the *Republican* appealed to
the people to suppress the City Abolition Society.
The streets were placarded calling a mass meeting
to assemble on the night of January 22.   The call
for the meeting was signed by the editors of the
daily papers, many prominent office-holders, and
aspirants for office.   It is noticeable that leaders of
anti-slavery mobs were always politicians—it was
politics rather than hatred of Abolitionists which
was the exciting cause.   On this point, Birney in his
second issue said :   "It is remarkable that no mob
has ever attacked the Abolitionists, except after special training by politicians, who have something to
hope for from the favor of the South.   The people
of whom mobs are composed care not a rush for the
abolition of slavery, and if left to themselves would
as soon think of attacking the Phrenologists as the
Abolitionists."*   The call was responded to by a large
and heterogeneous crowd at the court house.   Mayor
Davis presided.   Col. Hale of the militia, a livery-
stable keeper and ward politician, harangued the people.   He defamed Birney in a most scurrilous
manner, accusing him of amalgamation, incendia-
rism, treason, etc., etc., etc.   The mob element was
aroused to a state of fury, and were ready for "trea-
sons, strategems and spoils."   At this point, Birney,
who had the temerity to attend, arose and said :   "Mr.
President, can I be heard ?"   For a moment the
crowd was awed by his audacity, but only for a moment, for soon they burst forth with "Kill him,"
"Drag him out," and would have done so had it not

---

*Birney and His Times, p. 210, citing *Philanthropist* of January
8, 1836.

been for the interference of a few who shouted "Fair
play;" and through the influence of the gallant and
generous Surveyor-General Lytle, the mob was
quieted, and Birney was allowed to speak. By his
wit, bravery and good sense he completely disarmed
the crowd and was allowed to retire without mo-
lestation, and a night which promised to be filled
with violence and bloodshed passed quietly. But the
end was not yet. Soon after this meeting the office
of the *Philanthropist* was removed to Cincinnati,
where its publication was continued without moles-
tation till July 12, when at midnight a band of ruffians broke into the office, tore up the paper prepared
for the week's issue, poured out the ink, dismantled
the press, carrying parts of it outdoors. Notwithstanding this outrage occurred on one of the principal streets, creating a great noise, no policeman appeared; in fact, those usually on that beat had been
conveniently transferred to another, that very same
night.* Mr. Birney, nothing daunted, repaired his
presses and resumed the publication of his paper.
But his enemies were determined not to let him off
so easily. The daily press renewed its attacks
upon him, and a placard headed "Fugitive from
Justice," offering $100.00 reward for the delivery of
James G. Birney, and signed "Old Kentucky," was
posted on the streets. A mass meeting was called to
meet at lower market house at 6 P. M., July 23. This
meeting was remarkable for the number of eminent
and respectable men connected with it. About one
thousand assembled; of this number not more than
two hundred or three hundred belonged to the mob

*Narrative of Riotous Proceedings Against the Liberty of the
Press at Cincinnati, p. 12.

element. A committee of twelve was appointed to
confer with Mr. Birney, and request him to discon-
tinue the publication of his paper, as it was a constant menace to the peace of the city. This committee included men of the highest political and
social standing. The chairman was Judge Burnett
of the Supreme Court ; others were William Burke,
city postmaster, and David T. Disney, who had been
speaker of both houses of the Legislature and was
an influential politician ; the remainder were of like
respectability, men of wealth and prominent in business circles. Nine were Whigs, eight were members of the Protestant churches. For a week a
lively correspondence was kept up between the committee and Mr. Birney, representing the Ohio Anti-
Slavery Society ; but of course to no avail. Birney
and his friends were not made of the stuff that yields.
They planted themselves squarely on the Constitutional right of free speech and a free press, and there
they stood, "firm as mountains are." The papers
in the meantime kept up a regular fusillade of edito-
rials calculated to inflame the populace and incite
them to violence.* On Saturday morning the *Whig*
accompanied the publication of the report of the
committee with the following strain :

> "Lay on, McDuff, and d——d be he
> Who first cries, hold, enough!"

That same evening the leaders of the pro-slavery
element gathered a meeting, where it was resolved,
first, that the press should be destroyed, and second,
Mr. Birney should be notified to leave the city within
twenty-four hours.† That night a second attack

---

*For extracts from daily press, see Narrative of Riotous Proceed-
ings, p. 28, sq.
†Narrative of Riotous Proceedings, p. 39.

was made on the office of the *Philanthropist*. This time
the type was destroyed, the press dragged out and
down the street and dumped into the river, and the
office completely demolished. All this outrage was
perpetrated with the active connivance and assistance of the mayor of the city, whose duty it was,
presumably, to protect the property of the citizens.
After the mob had accomplished their work, the
mayor advised them to go home, as it was late,
"and they would disturb the rest of the sleeping citizens," by remaining longer. "The Abolitionists
themselves must be convinced by this time what
public sentiment is, and that it will not do any longer
to disregard it, or set it at naught." The mob then
dispersed. The publication of the paper was soon
resumed, as after the first attack, and from that time
no further trouble was experienced.

Prominent Abolitionists were often the occasion
of mob violence throughout the State, but according
to the testimony of William Birney, son of J. G.
Birney, their number and the mischief done were
often exaggerated. He says: " I have seen every
mob in Cincinnati between 1835 and 1848 and in
many other places of the State, and they have not
been, as a general thing, dangerous to life or limb,
or beyond the power of the police to suppress. They
made no martyrs, and seldom was anyone seriously
hurt. Abolition meetings were often assailed with
stones and other missiles, and it was considered a
practical joke to greet the lecturer with a volley of
rotten eggs."

Tar and feathers figured largely in pro-slavery
speeches, but only one Abolitionist was actually subjected to that indignity. Lecturers were often rudely

disturbed, and the meeting broken up, but very little
actual damage was done.*   That no more injury was
done by the pro-slavery mobs can be accounted for,
in part, at least, by the fact which has been alluded
to before, that they were usually instigated by politicians, who used them to secure southern favor.
Some fiery orator by his explosive rhetoric would
inflame the mob element to a state of perfect frenzy ;
but it had no depth of motive, and when confronted
by a bold, determined, but good-humored opponent,
their madness was   soon allayed, and it was not
surprising if they turned with cutting ridicule upon
the wily politician who had tried to use them as
his tools.

The pro-slavery sentiment expressed   itself not
only in unjust laws and social discriminations, and
lawless and illegal acts of violence, but penetrated
the courts of justice, and under the cloak of law,
worked mischief as despicable as any perpetrated by
a frenzied and lawless mob.   It is astonishing and
lamentable to see how· subservient to slave interests
the courts of Ohio were.   The South looked to them
for the protection of their properties which might be
found this side the river, and, to our shame be it said,
they were seldom disappointed.   It should be remarked to their extenuation that the courts could not
be asked to go behind the laws, and that it was the
duty of the judge simply to execute the law as he
found it, and if that law protected slavery rather than
freedom, it was not his fault if slavery obtained the
victory.

While this view may be true in a general sense,
yet in a free State it is reasonable to suppose that in

*Birney and His Times, p: 250.

cases of doubt the decision would be in favor of freedom rather than slavery. But in very many cases
we find that slavery had the "benefit of the doubt"
rather than freedom. Besides, a new and unprece-
dented interpretation of the law would be rendered,
or means still less unwarrantable would be used in
order to secure the interests of the slave-owners. In
the case of a servant of Harriet Beecher Stowe's, who
was suspected of being a runaway slave, a judge in
Cincinnati frankly acknowledged that it would be
impossible for her to obtain a fair hearing. A case
occurred in 1836, which will ever be memorable in
the annals of anti-slavery history, both for its fla-
grant violation of the Constitutional laws of the State
and the decisions of the Supreme Court of the State.
Matilda Lawrence was the slave daughter of a rich
Missouri planter. She was an octoroon and therefore nearly white, of striking beauty and most engag-
ing manners. Her neighbors, knowing her origin,
of course ostracised her from their society. Being
left to herself, she learned to read and spent most of
her time pouring over the books in her father's
library. Her father wishing to visit New York,
desired that she should accompany him as a nurse,
and wishing to avoid the "talk" which would naturally be aroused by traveling with such a beautiful
girl as a servant, he decided to take her as his
daughter. She was received with him at all hotels
and treated with all the deference due the daughter
of a rich southern planter. Her beauty attracted
many admirers, and the glimpse which she obtained
of social life made her unwilling to return to her
former isolated life on her father's plantation and in
all probability to the auction block after his death.

She quickly learned what her rights were in a free
State, and begged her father to make out her "free
papers," promising him in that case to go home and
serve him faithfully till his death. Her father became alarmed at this new freak of his beautiful slave
daughter, and not wishing to grant her request, decided at once to hasten home. When they reached
Cincinnati, Matilda was missing; she had taken
refuge in the home of a colored barber and after-
ward was found as a servant in the home of J. G.
Birney. Her father did not remain to look up his
"property," but continued his journey homeward.
Matilda became a great favorite in Mr. Birney's
household, no one ever dreaming but that she was a
white girl. She made her escape in May, and it
was the following March, nearly a year, before she
had occasion to have any fear of being betrayed.
In Cincinnati there was always a body of miscreants
whose business it was to capture runaway slaves, and
return them to their masters for the sake of the
reward offered. One of these human plunderers,
Riley by name, had spotted Matilda, and was watching his opportunity to seize her. Mr. Birney, knowing that she could not be legally remanded to slavery
since her master had voluntarily brought her into a
free State, yet suspicious of "the even poise of the
scales of justice, when they were held by the appoint-
ees of the slave power," made an attempt to conceal
her, but a warrant was sworn out by Riley for her
arrest, under the Fugitive Slave Law of 1793. Mr.
S. P. Chase, who had obtained the title of "Attorney
for Runaway Slaves," was retained by Mr. Birney to
defend her. The case was tried before Judge Este,
a Whig, who firmly believed in the Constitutional

right of slavery, and was equally firm in his belief
of the injustice of interfering with it. Mr. Chase, in
his defence, admitted the fact of her escape, but
argued that inasmuch as Matilda had been brought
into the State by her father, she could in no sense be
considered a fugitive, nor rightfully be claimed as
such under the provision of the Fugitive Slave Law
of 1793—a construction which was later universally
admitted to be true.* The outcome of the case we
will give in Chase's own words: "The cause was
heard by him with courtesy and fairness, but like
almost all lawyers, and indeed almost all men
at that time, he looked upon claims to slaves as more
entitled to favor than claims to liberty. He heard
me asserting what I believed to be the true principles
of Constitutional construction, and legal as well
as natural right, with the indifference with which
a kind-hearted professor of the Aristotelian philosophy may be supposed to have listened to
a youthful disciple of the doctrine of the earth's motion around the sun. On the other side, the appeals
of the council for the slave claimants were vehement
and passionate, and were supported by the prejudices
and sympathies of nearly the entire community. The
judge decided against the claim of Matilda, and she
was remanded into slavery. In thus deciding the
case, Judge Este acted contrary to the Constitutional
laws of the State—to the previous decision of the
State Supreme Court, and to the evidence then presented. (a) He pronounced Matilda colored when
the courts had declared white all those possessing

*This construction received judicial confirmation in the "Wat-
son case," see p. 140, and also case of Anderson vs. Poindexter,
6 Ohio Report, p. 622.

more than one-half white blood.*   (*b*) He considered her a slave even after touching Ohio soil, though
the Ordinance of 1787 and the Constitution of Ohio
prohibited slavery within the State.

(*c*) He assumed that she had escaped from Missouri into Ohio, though the evidence showed that she
had been brought there by her father.   (*d*) He had
only the affidavit of the slave hunter Riley to prove
that he was authorized to act as the Missouri planter's
agent.   That the court could so wantonly disregard
all these considerations and remand the unhappy girl
to the wretchedness of slavery, shows how completely under the influence of the slave power it must
have been.   The proximity of Kentucky made it
especially easy for slaves to make their escape into
Ohio, and afforded the lawyers and judges with political aspirations frequent opportunities to manifest
their deep respect for the ' peculiar institution' of
the South.   The disputed jurisdiction of the Ohio
river was a most fertile source for differences of
opinions, and gave the courts an excuse for many of
their pro-slavery decisions.   The friends of liberty
maintained that the territorial limits of Ohio extended at least to the low water mark of the river,
which is now considered correct, and consequently
boats anchored within this limit are in the State of
Ohio and subject to its laws.

But we find that the judiciary, while repeatedly
avowing the local character of slavery, and the freedom of slaves as soon as they entered a free State

*Polly Grey vs. the State of Ohio, Hammonds Ohio Reports,
4:354. This decision was confirmed in case of Jeffries vs. Aukerry,
11 Ohio Reports, p. 372, and the case of Anderson vs. Millikin, 9
Ohio Reports, p. 568.

by the consent of their masters, made exceptions in the case of slaves escaping from boats on the river, even when tied to the bank and within the low water.

A case occurred in 1845 which will illustrate this point. A boat having a slave on board was fastened to the bank of the river. In the morning, the slave, Watson by name, disappeared, and in the evening was found strolling along the docks. He was captured and papers at once made out for taking him out of the State as a fugitive slave. S. P. Chase defended him, and made the same plea as in the case of Matilda. He claimed that slavery was a local institution, and that a slave taken beyond the influence of the laws which supported slavery became free.

Judge Reed in his decision fully sanctioned this principle, and the logic of his position would have led him to the inevitable conclusion that Watson was a free man and therefore entitled to his liberty. "But he avoided this conclusion by declaring that the Ohio river was for purposes of navigation as much under the slave laws of Kentucky as under the free laws of Ohio, entirely ignoring the fact that Watson, when arrested, was not on board, but on the landing, and was not trying to escape, and had the courts favored as decidedly the rights of men as they did the claims of the masters, without doubt Watson would have been discharged."*

Cases might be multiplied, many fold, which would illustrate the attitude of the judiciary toward slavery, but enough has been said to show the position taken by it. It is an ineffaceable stigma upon the honor of

* Chase to J. T. Trowbridge, March 19, 1845, cited in Warden's Life of Chase, p. 309.

Ohio that the courts should have allowed themselves to be so prostrated to the service of slavery.

By way of explaining the perverse action of the judiciary at times, certain facts must be considered. First: Courts of law are always conservative. They are expected to deal entirely with facts ; they study the real and not the ideal ; they are concerned about what is, and not what ought to be ; they stand for what is permanent, uniform and just in society ; they are created for the purpose of protecting the citizen in his personal and property rights.

Second: Judges who are elected by the popular vote are naturally ambitious for the future and greater honors ; they must be careful to reflect public sentiment, and not be too far in advance of it. If the mass of the people were so far in favor of slavery as to demand the protection of its interests, it could not be expected that the judges would hold opinions very different, and if they should chance to render a questionable judgment, it was only the prominence of their position which rendered it the more conspicuous. But when the general sentiment changed, and the North realized something of the power which slaveocracy had over them, then the courts changed too, and in the later years of the struggle there were on the Supreme Bench earnest, conscientious men who never catered to the interests of slave-owners, but were always ready to grant protection to the unfortunate negro to the very limit of the law.

Having considered at some length the pro-slavery sentiment in Ohio and its forms of expression, we will be glad to give a glance at the growth and manifestation of anti-slavery principles in the State.

While there were always in Ohio those who were

ready to subserve the interests of slavery, there were
also those equally ready to advance the interests of
freedom. In the earliest period of the State's history,
there was a small but determined band of men thoroughly imbued with anti-slavery convictions. Among
the most active we find the name of Obed Denham,
whom we think worthy of special mention. He was
the proprietor of the village of Bethel, Claremont
county, and laid it out in 1799. He was a native of
Kentucky and a member of the Baptist church, and
in donating two lots to that denomination, he included in the deed of conveyance the following
record: "I also give two lots in said town, numbers
80 and 108, for the use of the regular Baptist church
who do not hold slaves, nor commune at the Lord's
table with those who practice such tyranny over their
fellow creatures."*

With Denham came a number of Abolitionists and
they established a settlement in Claremont county.
Another name among the pioneers in anti-slavery
work is that of Rev. Dyer Burgess, pastor of the
Presbyterian church at West Union, Adams county,
from 1800 to 1840. During the entire forty years his
sermons were uncompromisingly against slavery. In
1817, he began to refuse communion to slave-
holders. Others among the early workers were Rev.
John Rankin, Rev. Samuel Crothers, Benjamin
Lundy and many others who waged an uncondi-
tional warfare against the evil in any of its manifes-
tations. But in the main their work was isolated,
without any well-laid and concerted plan of action;
there was no organized work till 1835, when the
Ohio Anti-Slavery Society was formed. Previous to

* Birney's Life of Birney. p. 164.

that time there had been local societies in many
places, each with its individual name and constitution,
entirely independent of the others, but all working
with a common purpose for the immediate abolition
of African slavery. A local society was formed in
the early part of the century at Ripley, another at
Mt. Pleasant in 1815 by Benjamin Lundy; at West
Union in 1818, by Rev. Dyer Burgess; at Zanesville
in 1826, and the list could be greatly extended, but
enough has been given to show that even in the early
history of Ohio the friends of abolition were "up
and doing," zealous in their efforts to hasten the day
when human bondage would be forever banished
from the country. A growing conviction was felt
that much strength was lost in the lack of united
action, and that the formation of a State society to
which all local societies would be auxiliary, would
render the work far more efficient and enthusiastic.

To this end a convention was called to meet at
Putnam, April 22, 1835, and "all persons who advocated the principles of immediate emancipation
without expatriation" were invited to attend.* At
first there was an unwillingness on the part of local
societies to relinquish their name and independence
and date their origin from the formation of the State
society. Nevertheless, in answer to the call, 110
delegates representing twenty-six counties, besides
the corresponding members, assembled at Putnam.
The Ohio Anti-Slavery Society was organized, with
Hon. Leicester King as president.

The members declared their purpose to be "to
labor by every lawful and peaceable means for
'emancipation—immediate, total and universal.'"

---

* Proceedings of Convention, p. 3

After the formation of the State society, local societies multiplied rapidly, increasing from 20 in 1835
to 120 in 1836, with a membership varying from 11
to 940.* In five years, the number of societies had
increased to 251.† These societies were untiring in
their efforts to keep before the public a knowledge
of the evils of slavery. They circulated leaflets,
published newspapers, invoked the aid of the pulpit,
sent their agents and lecturers everywhere throughout the State, organizing societies and advocating
the principles of abolition. The press was perhaps
the most efficient agent in the dissemination of anti-
slavery principles, and to Ohio belongs the honor of
being the birth-place of the first anti-slavery news-
paper published in the United States. It was the
Philanthropist, and was published at Mt. Pleasant
in 1817–18, by Charles Osborne. He was assisted
by Benjamin Lundy, who afterwards removed to
East Tennessee and published there the *Genius of
Universal Emancipation*. He was instrumental in
organizing hundreds of anti-slavery societies in Ohio
and other States. In 1823 he visited Boston, and
there met William Lloyd Garrison, then a young
man of twenty-three, who soon enlisted with him in
the great work to which he had so intensely com-
mitted himself.‡ He was often called the "Father
of Abolition."

The societies in Ohio did more than talk and
preach—they lived out their convictions in "deeds."
They not only condemned slavery, but many refused
to purchase the products of slavery, on the ground

* First Annual Report of the Ohio Anti-Slavery Society, p. 20.
† Fifth Annual Report of the Ohio Anti-Slavery Society.
‡ Life of Garrison, 1:92.

that it was inconsistent to condemn the slave-holder and then buy the fruits of slave labor, which alone made slave-holding profitable. At the convention at Putnam in 1835, the members declared that they would practically testify against slavery by giving their uniform preference to the products of free labor.*

Two years later (1837), at the second anniversary of the Ohio Anti-Slavery Society, it was resolved to urge upon all friends of abolition in the State "to enter into and promote, as far as practicable, the culture of the sugar beet, as a means of diminishing the extensive use of the products of slave labor."† The inconsistency of using the fruits of slave labor took a strong hold on many of the Abolitionists throughout the country. In New York and Philadelphia, wholesale houses were established which dealt exclusively in "free labor products." They bought their sugar and cotton from non-slaveholding planters. Refineries and several looms were established which worked up the raw material without the help of slave labor. In Ohio, the Quakers were especially rigid in their purpose to abstain from the use of everything which they knew had been produced by slave labor. They were as fixed in their opposition as ever our forefathers were in abstaining from the use of tea, on which a tax had been paid to the English government.

In 1846 a convention was held at Salem, Indiana, of all those interested in the subject of free labor. It was largely attended by prominent anti-slavery workers from Ohio. At this convention the organ-

* Proceedings of Convention, p. 11.
† Second Annual Report Ohio Anti-Slavery Society, p. 14.

ization of the Free Produce Association was effected.
It was resolved to raise a fund of $3,000 to be loaned
for five years without interest, to some suitable person, to enable him to open a wholesale house for free
labor deposits, at Cincinnati. Levi Coffin of New
Port, Indiana, a Quaker and staunch friend of fugitive slaves, was chosen for this purpose.

He opened his depository the following year, with
a stock of goods "warranted" strictly free from
slave labor, purchased at New York and Philadelphia.

An agent was sent to the South to see that the
arrangements made with the cotton planters were
strictly carried out. A cotton-gin was purchased
and shipped to a planter in Mississippi who owned
no slaves and bought his cotton from small farmers.
This gin became notorious in that part of the country as the "abolition gin." The cotton was hauled
to Memphis and delivered to a non-slaveholding com-
mission merchant, who shipped it to Cincinnati on
boats which employed no slaves. This cotton was
delivered to Mr. Coffin without a stroke of slave
labor upon it.*

The Abolitionists who confined themselves to free
labor products did so at no small inconvenience, and
often at considerable pecuniary sacrifice. Their
willingness to make such sacrifices is surely indica-
tive of the deep sincerity of their convictions, and
though many, now as then, may be tempted to call
them fanatics, yet no one can help admiring their
conscientious determination to stand to their convictions and not "trespass in the accursed thing."
Their life was a continued testimony against the in-

* Reminiscences of Levi Coffin, pp. 272 and 278.

justice and wickedness of chattel slavery, and an un-
failing stimulous toward arousing and strengthening
public sentiment against the institution.

For the first forty years of this century the anti-
slavery people in Ohio, as in other States, used only
moral weapons in their efforts to put away the great
evil. But the rapidly developing political character
which slavery assumed compelled many thoughtful
men to consider the coming necessity of resorting to
political agencies in order to meet political aggres-
sions; moral means seemed quite inadequate to
grapple with " wickedness in high places."

The thought of a new political party which should
be formed on purely abolition principles, was at first
extremely repugnant to the main body of anti-slavery
workers in Ohio. In 1837, and again in 1838, the
Anti-Slavery Society, in its annual State convention,
declared itself in most unequivocal terms against any
measure looking toward the formation of a separate
political party. They argued that their motives
would be misinterpreted; that they would be considered as political aspirants seeking official honors;
that they would be tempted to resort to the ordinary
machinery of partisan warfare, and thus prevent the
very reformation in public sentiment which they so
much desired to accomplish; that the channels then
opened to reach the ears and hearts of the law-makers
would be cut off, and all attempts to conciliate their
opponents would be useless; internal dissensions
would likely arise which would divide their forces,
and thus the great moral question of slavery would
be subverted to the channels of party politics.* The
following year the Abolitionists of the Western Re-

* Third Annual Report of Ohio Anti-Slavery Society in Ohio.

serve, the nursery of abolition principles, assembled in convention at Cleveland, October 23, 1839, at which time they again vigorously denounced the attempt to form a third party, on the ground that it would restrict their efforts : that they could then only oppose slavery in the territo.... and District of Columbia, and in the admission of new States. On the contrary, as an anti-slavery society they could oppose it anywhere and in any form. They said, " Our object is not the formation of a new party ; we repudiate the name party."*

The sentiments expressed in the above declarations probably represent quite accurately the feeling of nearly all the anti-slavery people in Ohio in 1839.

The next year (1840), through the influence of Myron Holley, Gerrit Smith and others who favored political action, a convention was called to meet at Albany, April 1. Only six States were represented, and but seventeen delegates outside of New York State. This convention put in nomination for President, J. G. Birney, and for Vice-President, Thomas Earle of Pennsylvania. Mr. Birney, though a resident of Ohio and, as we have seen, a most prominent, self-sacrificing and zealous worker in the anti-slavery cause, yet in the following fall election received only 903 votes from his associates in the State.† The great majority of the Abolitionists still clung to their old parties. Those who supported Birney represented the extreme radical wing of the anti-slavery class, who with Garrison verily thought slavery must be overthrown at any price, and who were willing to sacrifice party, church and Union,

* Life of Garrison, II., p. 314.
† Stanwood's History of Presidential Elections, p. 138.

and to subject the country to the evils and terrors of a civil war, if need be, to accomplish their purpose; while the majority, like Chase and Giddings, were equally earnest in their purpose, but hoped to secure the same end by "moral suasion," or through the co-operation of the old parties.

The sudden death of General Harrison so soon after his inauguration, and the succession of Tyler to the Presidential chair, gave a great impulse to the Liberty party. Many Whigs, despairing of ever obtaining any efficient anti-slavery legislation from their party, now abandoned it, and joined the ranks of the Liberty party. Among the most prominent of these recruits was S. P. Chase, who devoted his time and his great talents to its advancement. Although his broad nature never allowed his adherence to party to prevent him from adopting any course which, in his opinion, would best promote the interests of freedom, he was active in calling a State convention at Columbus in 1841, and was the author of the resolutions then adopted and of the address to the people.* The convention nominated for Governor, Leicester King, the first president of the State Anti-Slavery Society. He polled 5,305 votes, an increase over the number given for Birney the year before (1840) of 4,402.

It is not our purpose to trace the history of the party, except so far as it indicates the increasing anti-slavery sentiment in the State. Its members, though undoubtedly sincere in their convictions, yet in certain cases acted (from the standpoint of expediency) in a most impolitic way. For instance, in 1844, in common with their associates in other States, they again supported Birney for President, which

---

* Schucker's Life of Chase, p. 69.

resulted in the defeat of Henry Clay and their own
anti-slavery objects, by the election of a pro-slavery
candidate, James K. Polk.   Had the votes of even
half the Liberty party in New York been given to
Clay, his election would unquestionably have been
secured, and the admission of Texas as a slave State
would have been at least postponed.   By the time of
the next Presidential election (1848), the Liberty
party had been absorbed into the more practical Free
Soil party.

Then was the opportunity for the Abolitionists to
perform their greatest service for the negro.   We
have already given the account of the way the Free
Soilers obtained the balance of power in the State
Legislature, and thus secured the repeal of the
" Black Laws."   But in this the honor does not so
much belong to the Free Soilers as to the two independents whom they read out of their party, and
who, by their alliance with the Democrats, accomplished the long-worked-for repeal.   While the
Abolitionists were sometimes apparently blinded to
their own interests, and some may be tempted to censure their want of wise " policy," yet no one will
withhold all honor to the sincerity of their convictions, to the persistence with which they defended
them, and to the valuable service which they rendered in the final overthrow of slavery.   I think,
however, that all will agree in the opinion that S. P.
Chase took a more practical view when he refused
to be strictly bound by any political ties or methods,
that he might be free to adopt any measures which
seemed to him most expedient for advancing the
cause of freedom.   As a result of his position, he
was instrumental in the repeal of the " Black Laws,"

and was sent to the United States Senate by the Democratic party, where his voice and vote were always given to restrict the evils of human bondage.

In reviewing the slavery sentiment in Ohio, we find that, at the beginning, there were only scattered individuals who were thoroughly imbued with a hatred of the monster, on the one hand, and, on the other hand, only a few who were pronounced in their pro-slavery views, while the great majority were, to a certain extent, indifferent to either side. This class, however, generally inclined to the anti-slavery side to the extent of desiring slavery restricted to its then existing limits. As the institution became more and more a political and industrial one, and the South, to secure increased political power and new industrial opportunities, sought to extend its limits farther and farther, the people of Ohio "lined up" for the impending struggle. Those whose social and economic interests had been linked with the South, became more and more pronounced in their pro-slavery views, while those who by hereditary training and personal observation had learned to look upon chattel slavery with abhorrence, sought with an increasing zeal to assert their convictions, and to gain recruits for their ranks. The time soon came when the indifferent must "take sides."

Very few joined the radical pro-slavery party, but every year, after the organization of the State Anti-Slavery Society in 1835, brought an increasing number to the ranks of the Abolitionists. The majority, while they could not accept their extreme views, yet always stood squarely opposed to any further extension of slavery. These determined the politics of the State, and placed Ohio in the front rank of States who stood for restricting the extension of slavery, and for mitigating its evils by every possible means in harmony with the Constitution and the preservation of the Union. This position of Ohio is fully confirmed by her action respecting the admission ot new States. In 1820, the Legislature requested, by joint resolution, their senators and representatives at Washington to use their influence to exclude slavery from Missouri,* and twenty-five years later (1845) it protested against the admission of Texas as a slave State.† It followed the same course respecting Oregon in 1847,‡ and again similar resolutions were passed in 1848, regarding all territory acquired from Mexico,§ and the same precedent was followed when Kansas asked for admission in 1856.‖

There is one more feature of the anti-slavery sentiment in Ohio which must be considered, viz., that of its relation to fugitive slaves. The scope of the present work does not permit an exhaustive account of runaway slaves in their flight into and through the State, nor of that unique and mysterious, but effective institution known as the Under-Ground Railroad. But no account of the negro in Ohio could lay any claim to completeness, which did not make some mention of his unfortunate brother, who, impelled by the love of liberty, attempted by his cunning and bravery to cross the State in search of freedom.

———

*Senate Journal, 16th Cong., 1st Session, p. 136.
†House Docs. No. 65, 28th Cong., 2d Session, vol. 2.
‡House Docs. No. 89, 29th Cong., 2d Session, vol. 4.
§House Mis. Docs. No. 84, 30th Cong., 1st Session.
‖Sen. Mis. Docs. No. 49, 34th Cong., 1st Session, vol. 1.

During the earliest years of American slavery it was no uncommon occurrence for slaves to run away. It was in the very nature of the system that it should be so. Southern slave-owners were thoroughly alive to this fact, and it will be remembered that as early as 1787, in the Philadelphia Convention, delegates from the South insisted that their States would never consent to enter the Union unless some Constitutional provision should be made for the surrender of such runaways. The Northern States yielded, and a few years later the Constitutional law requiring the rendition of all "persons held in service or labor" and escaping from one State into another, was supplemented by statute legislation. This latter law is familiarly known as the Fugitive Slave Law of 1793. It provided for the surrender of all fugitives to their owner, or agent, when their title to them had been attested before any United States Court in the State, or before any magistrate in the county where the arrest was made; and imposed a fine of $500 upon any one obstructing the arrest or aiding in the escape of the prisoner.

This was the National law under which fugitive slaves were apprehended and returned to their masters until the passage of the famous Fugitive Slave Law of 1850.

During the early part of the century instances of running away were not at all frequent. But during the second war with Great Britain, not a few slaves made their escape and ultimately found their way into Canada, and there learned that they were free men in a free country. Some of these were not slow in hastening back to their southern homes to tell the "glad tidings" to their brothers in bondage that in

the North was a land of freedom. Such news naturally spread rapidly among the slaves, and by clan-
destine interviews with these bold fellows who had
generously dared to face the awful consequences of
a capture, and had returned to tell the glad news,
and by occasional hints dropped by some northern
travelers in the South, the great fact was confirmed
that in some north land freedom was to be found.

From the same sources they gained a knowledge
of the direction and routes to be followed, the dangers
to be encountered, and the assistance which could
be expected on the way to the "promised land" of
liberty. The close proximity of Ohio to the slave
States on the south and to Canada on the north,
offered superior opportunities for slaves, especially
from Kentucky, to effect an escape. They crossed
the Ohio river at many points, but generally at or
near Cincinnati, because of the number of Abolitionists living at that point, from whom they would be
sure of a hearty welcome. Crossing the State they
left it for Canada at any of the lake ports where
passage could be secured with some friendly captain.

From the beginning, Sandusky took rank as one of
the most favorable ports for embarkation. According to Rush R. Sloane, one of the most zealous and
self-sacrificing friends of the negro, and a resident
of Sandusky, we learn that the first runaway slave
reached that city in 1820. He was closely followed
by his master, but was taken in charge by a generous
captain who concealed him in his boat, and finally
landed him safely on the Canadian shore.* This

*Address delivered by Rush R. Sloane before the Firelands His-
torical Society at Milan, February 22, 1888. Printed in the following May issue of the Magazine of Western History, and also
in vol. 5 (new series) of the Firelands Pioneer.

was probably one of the first, if not the very first slave to make his escape through Ohio. It was not, however, by any means the last. They quickly learned that although the way to freedom was beset with dangers and suffering, yet there were friends scattered along the route, who were ever ready to lend sympathy and aid to the wearied fugitive.

The Underground Railroad was the popular designation given to the efforts, more or less systematic and co-operative, made in behalf of the hapless fugitives by their northern sympathizers. The origin of the name is disputed, but there seems to be good reason for accepting the one given below as substantially correct. In 1831, a Kentucky slave, Tice Davids, ran away. His absence was soon discovered, and he was closely pursued by his infuriated master. Coming to the Ohio river opposite the village of Ripley, "Tice" boldly jumped in and swam across. The master, after some delay in finding a skiff, followed, keeping his eye on him till he reached the shore, when he suddenly disappeared, and his owner never saw him again. The inhabitants of Ripley claimed to have seen nothing of the fugitive, and the master, after searching in vain every possible opening or hiding place along the river bank, finally gave up the search, remarking that the "nigger must have gone off by an underground road."

At this time the advent of steam railroads was creating a tremendous excitement, and this name naturally soon changed to the Underground Railroad.*

———

*The origin of the name as given in the text is that given by Mr. Sloane referred to above, in his address before the Firelands Historical Society. In a letter to me (dated December 24, 1894), Mr. Sloane writes as follows concerning it: "About 1834 a col-

Though the above explanation may not be historically correct in every particular, yet it seems probable that the name arose from this or some similar incident.

The organization of the Anti-Slavery Society in 1836, and the rapid increase of local societies which immediately followed, gave a great impetus to the " business " all along the " line." In fact, previous to this year very few fugitives had escaped into Ohio. We cannot be far from the truth if we say that the Underground Railroad began its operations in Ohio simultaneously with the establishment of the Anti-Slavery Society. The two always worked in harmony together, and the operators of the one were generally active members of the other. One of the earliest and most successful " conductors " of the " road " was John Rankin. He was especially active in the convention at Putnam, 1835, and took a prominent part in effecting the organization of the Anti-

ored man named Elijah Brown came to Sandusky and soon after contracted for 50 acres of land a few miles out of town. It turned out that he was an escaped slave from Kentucky, and his master was the same who had owned "Tice." After Tice's escape, and on his master's return from his unsuccessful pursuit, he told the story as I give it, and Brown heard it, and after his arrival here, he told how he escaped by the Underground Railroad, and when asked to explain, told the story as given by his master."

Eben M. Pettit, in his "Sketches on the History of the Underground Railroad," p. 35, gives quite a different origin to the name. He ascribes it to an incident which happened in Washington, D. C., in 1839, and claims that the term "Underground Railroad" was first used at that time. A young negro was caught lurking around the Capitol, and when questioned as to how he came there, said he had been sent North by a "railroad which went underground all the way to Boston." It seems obvious that the expression could not have been original with him, and that Mr. Pettit must be mistaken in his conclusion.

Slavery Society. Henry Ward Beecher, when asked
after the war, " Who abolished slavery?" is said to
have answered, " Rev. John Rankin and his sons
did."* This humorous exaggeration of his services
indicates the prominent position which he held in
anti-slavery circles. He was the pastor of the Presbyterian church in Ripley for thirty-three years. His
house was situated on a hill three hundred feet high,
overlooking the Ohio river, and could be seen for a
great distance from the Kentucky side. The light
which every night shone from the windows became
the beacon light for thousands of fugitives pursuing
their journey to the north land of freedom. Rankin's
home was one of the first and most frequented
" depots " along the route. " George Harris " and
"Eliza" of " Uncle Tom's Cabin " fame stopped
here, and after receiving food and dry clothing were
hurried on to another station of the Underground
Railroad.

None of the earnest, self-sacrificing men who were
engaged in advancing the cause of freedom can de-
serve more well-merited praise than Levi Coffin. He
was kind, shrewd, good-natured and an indefatiga-
ble worker; there was no denial which his great,
generous heart was not willing to make for the sake
of the oppressed race. At his home in Newport,
Indiana, and later in Cincinnati, any man, white or
black, who was in distress, found a " safe retreat."
It is estimated that for thirty-three years he was instrumental in the escape of one hundred slaves
yearly.† Among other homes which were always

* Life of J. G. Birney, p. 168.
† Lecture on Underground Railroad, delivered in Cleveland,
January, 1895, by Prof. J. H. Fairchild of Oberlin College.

open to the weary fugitive were those of Leicester King, Elizur Wright, John Sloane, David Hudson, the founder of the present village of that name; Owen Brown, the father of the immortal John Brown; J. G. Birney, Asa Cady and many others equally prominent whom space alone prevents our mentioning.

The amount of printed data concerning the *modus operandi* of this unique and interesting railroad is extremely limited. There was no formal organization, no election of officers, no annual meetings, no conferences respecting "rates," and no printed reports, and yet there were "stations" and "conductors," and the number of passengers transported over the "road" during its history amounted to thousands. The "stations" were generally equipped with a secret chamber, where the frightened, footsore fugitive was safely secreted from the pursuing slave hunter. Such a room, with which the writer is familiar, was built into the wall and in connection with the chimney, which served as an entrance for light and air. The door opened into the dark cellar, and was so carefully constructed as to utterly deceive the eye. In other "stations" a harmless-looking bookcase concealed an entrance into a closet where three or four men could be securely tucked away. The conductor to be successful must possess bravery, tact and shrewdness. He must be ready to devise "ways and means" for throwing an angry and inquisitive slave hunter off the track. He must be close-mouthed, and an adept at telling the truth without giving any information. The Quakers possessed these necessary requisites in a remarkable degree. Their kindly good humor would often so entirely disarm the pursuer that his victim would make good his escape.

The "stations" were generally from ten to thirty miles apart, and the fugitives would either be directed to the next one or carried in a covered wagon. Their safe transportation was often arduous and perilous. The greatest precaution must be taken to prevent arousing any suspicion, for there were always people who were ever on the alert to discover a fugitive, and make trouble for their friends who might aid them in their flight. Consequently, they usually ran "night trains," avoiding main roads as much as possible. Very often the nights were dark and stormy and the roads rough and unfamiliar. The various strategems resorted to by white sympathizers are manifold and very interesting.

At one time in Cincinnati there was a company of twenty-eight fugitives driven through the streets in broad day-light in closed coaches. They formed a procession as if going to a funeral, and drove solemnly along the road leading to the next station.*

At another time, in the same city, a number of fugitives were hiding, not daring to venture further because the slave-hunters were watching every street leading out of the city. It was decided that it would be best to send them out during the day, without any attempt at concealment. Accordingly, the males were disguised as females and the females as males, in clothing of bright color, such as the well-to-do colored people affected, and seated in elegant carriages, they drove boldly through the streets. Those who were watching for a company of miserably dressed fugitives never suspicioned these fine "turn-

---

* Reminiscences of Levi Coffin, p. 308.

outs," for it was common for the colored gentry of the city to ride out in this style.*   In 1860, Levi Coffin was advised that a box had been expressed to him from Nashville, Tennessee, and he was requested to call for it as soon as it should arrive in Cincinnati.   He immediately called at the express office and inquired if there was a box there for him. The agent replied that a box had been shipped to him, but at Seymour, Indiana, it burst open, and out rolled a "nigger."   The poor fellow had hired someone to box him up and express him to Mr. Coffin, knowing that if he was once under his hospitable roof he would be well cared for and helped on his way to the land of liberty.   In 1855, another fugitive, who had succeeded in getting as far as Shelby, Ohio, and being hard pressed by his pursuers, who had seemingly cut off every avenue of escape, had himself put into a coffin and shipped to Sandusky.   It was nothing but a rough box, full of knot holes, and around the head shavings were crowded.   After a two hours' ride the coffin was taken in charge by a friend in Sandusky, and taken to his home and opened.   "The eyes were blood-shot, the mouth was foaming, and the poor fellow was nearly dead."   In a few hours, however, the " corpse " was in an exceedingly lively and healthful condition.†

Many similar instances might be given, but these are enough to show to what unique and sometimes perilous expedients the negroes and their friends would resort to in order to elude the vigilance of wicked men-hunters.

* Reminiscences of Levi Coffin, p. 315.
† Address by Rush R. Sloane referred to above.

It will be interesting to notice the different railroad lines which traversed the State during the years of fugitive experiences.   Before 1836 there was little known of the Underground Railroad among the slaves.   They had learned to distinguish in a vague way the difference between slave and free States, and that somewhere to the North there was a land of freedom.   They knew nothing of its distance, nor of the dangers which lay between them and the promised land of refuge.   Of helps by the way, or of different "routes" up to this time they were ignorant, only as they had heard hints, from different sources. With the North star as their guide, and the burning love of liberty in their hearts, the "runaways" trudged on, in weariness and trepidation, along the rough, unknown and dangerous road.   They were the pioneers who blazed the path from bondage to liberty, which should serve their fellows in the coming years.   They were quick to learn, and the slaves soon knew the names and places of certain Abolitionists who would help them, and accordingly directed their footsteps to the first house where they could find care and protection.   Here the route which offered the least obstacles was chosen, and the way definitely mapped out for them.

Mr. Coffin, who certainly is authority on the subject, informs us that a favorite " route " from Cincinnati was by way of Spartansburg, Greenville, through Mercer county, to Sandusky, thence to Malden on the Canadian shore.   This was known as the Greenville and Sandusky route.   Another from Cincinnati followed the road through Hamilton, Elktown to Eaton, then turned to the Northwest, leaving the State near Paris; then to Newport, Indiana, where it converged at the house of Mr. Coffin with two Indiana lines, thence crossed the State to Michigan and Detroit. The Western Reserve was fairly honeycombed with routes leading to various lake ports. The people of the Reserve entertained strong anti-slavery convictions, but not of the radical type. Garrison's idea that the " Constitution was a covenant with death and a league with hell" found little sympathy with them. Their sentiments were more perfectly represented by Wade and Giddings in the National Congress, and by Morse and Townshend in the State Legislature. They were always ready to lend a helping hand to fleeing fugitives, and the boast was once made that a fugitive could not be captured in Cleveland.

The villages of Oberlin and Hudson were among the most prominent stations. Oberlin College took such a leading part in the anti-slavery work that a violent antipathy was aroused against the institution among the opposers of the work, which resulted in a serious discussion in favor of revoking its character. In 1843 a bill was actually introduced into the Legislature for that purpose. At first, the House was favorably disposed toward it; it was finally decided, by a vote of 36 to 29, to indefinitely postpone final action.* Though the citizens of Oberlin always did their best to prevent the capture of a fugitive, they did not as a rule believe in encouraging or aiding slaves to escape. Fugitives who found their way there were sure of finding food and shelter and carefully protected from the pursuers till some captain could be found who would be kind enough to "look the other way" while they were taken aboard

* House Journal, 1842–3, p. 227.

his boat, and safely landed at some Canadian port. In 1845, Calvin Fairbanks went to Kentucky for the purpose of assisting slaves in making their escape. He was detected, arrested, convicted and sentenced to eleven years in the Kentucky penitentiary. The Oberlin people sympathized with him in his misfortunes, but did not approve his course.* Prof. W. H. Siebert, who has made extensive investigations in the history of the Underground Railroad, says in respect to the extent of the railroad in Ohio, that there were not less than twenty-three ports of entry along the river. Thirteen of these admitted slaves from 275 miles of Kentucky shore and ten from 150 miles of the Virginia border. From these ports they took a zigzag course to the five harbors on Lake Erie. These were Toledo, Sandusky, Cleveland, Fairport (near Painesville) and Ashtabula.† To these I think should be added Huron, Vermillion and Lorain, thus making eight in all. Prof. Siebert, after making a careful measurement of the railroad lines already unearthed, estimates that there must have been between 2,800 and 3,000 miles in Ohio. The counties having the greatest number were, Trumbull, 153 miles; Richland, 123 miles; Huron and Belmont, 120 miles each; Ashtabula and Jefferson, 117 miles each; Lorain, 108 miles, and Mahoning, 105 miles. It is worth noticing that four of these counties were in the Western Reserve.

Operating the Underground Railroad was often attended with great danger to the operators. The

---

* Fairchild's History of the Oberlin Colony, p. 227.

† "The Underground Railroad in Ohio." An article by Prof. W. H. Siebert published in the February issue of the *Archæologist*, 1895.

laws were very severe against harboring or aiding in any way a fugitive slave, and anyone detected in the offense would be heavily fined. An illustration in point is the pathetic case of John Vanzandt, the original "Honest Van Trompe" of "Uncle Tom's Cabin." Returning to his farm from the Cincinnati market in 1842, he overtook nine fugitive slaves, who importuned him for a ride. His big heart moved with pity for them in their pitiful condition, and he undertook to take them to Lebanon or Springfield. He was met by a gang of ruffians about fifteen miles north of Cincinnati, who attempted to seize them— and succeeded, excepting one, who jumped out and fled. On "double quick" time they hustled them back to Kentucky. They were tried for abduction, but the temper of the court and the times was such that they were acquitted. Then followed a suit against Vanzandt by Jones, the owner of the slaves, for aiding them to escape. He was tried under the Fugitive Slave Law of 1793, and notwithstanding no evidence was presented which proved that Vanzandt knew that they were fugitives, he was convicted. The damages, cost and fine assessed by the court amounted to $1,200, which exhausted his entire property,* and thus rendered an honest, generous-hearted farmer penniless in order to meet the penalty for the atrocious crime—humaneness.

However skilled the regular officers of the law, assisted by a large corps of self-appointed officers, might be in ferreting out fleeing fugitives and returning them to their owners—and however ready the courts were to punish anyone who could be shown to have harbored, or in any way aided them in their

* Warden's Life of Chase, p. 297.

flight, slaves continued to escape to Ohio in ever-increasing numbers.   Early in 1839, Kentucky sent a deputation to the Ohio Legislature, praying that body to pass more stringent measures for punishing evil-minded persons for enticing away and "sheltering their slaves, and to provide more efficient means for recapturing and bringing away absconding slaves." The deputation was received with distinguished consideration and courtesy by the Legislature. They arrived on the twenty-sixth of January; by the twenty-eighth of the next month the Legislature had prepared and passed the "Fugitive Slave Law of 1839." The conciliatory and apologetic tone of the preamble indicates that the legislators might have had some fears of its favorable acceptance by all the citizens of the State. The preamble is as follows :

WHEREAS, The United States Constitution states that no fugitive from labor shall escape from the service due, and,

WHEREAS, The laws of Ohio are inadequate to carry out such provisions, and,

WHEREAS, Those reaping the benefits of the United States Constitution are in duty bound to fulfill the obligations imposed upon them by that instrument, and

WHEREAS, It is the deliberate conviction of this General Assembly that the Constitution can only be sustained, as it was formed, by a spirit of just compromise, therefore—

Then followed the provisions of the law, which were in substance as follows :   (a) The master or his agent is authorized to apply to any judge or justice of the peace, or mayor of any municipal corporation, who upon such application shall issue a warrant to any sheriff in the State, directing him to arrest a fugitive, and bring him before any judge in the county in which he shall be arrested, and if the claimant can prove to the satisfaction of the court that he has a legal right to the fugitive, then a certificate shall be issued authorizing his removal from the State.

(*b*) It was enjoined that if anyone should prevent or hinder the execution of a warrant or the removal of a negro from the State, or aid in his rescue, he shall be liable to fine to any sum not exceeding five hundred dollars and imprisonment not over sixty days.

(*c*) The same penalty shall be imposed upon anyone who shall entice or even advise a slave to run away, or aid him in his escape, by food, money or conveyance.*

It seems very clear that such a law must have been dictated by Southern slave-owners, in that every facility is offered for securing a warrant, and for the execution of it. If there was any reason to believe that one official would refuse a warrant, then application was made to another whose sympathies were known to be with the South.

So bold did the slaveocracy become that it not only presumed to dictate to the Legislature of Ohio what laws should be passed, but even attempted in many cases to interfere and direct the execution of these laws. An incident occurred this year which well illustrates how lawless and wanton was the spirit with which the southern slave-holders pursued their fugitive slaves, and equally outraged the moral

*Laws of Ohio, 37:38.

sentiment of the people and defied the dignity and decisions of the courts.   In Marion a negro was arrested on the claim that he was an escaped slave.   The court decided that there was not evidence sufficient to hold him, and declared him free.   At this announcement, his pursuers, at the point of pistols, knives and dirks, and defying the court and bystanders, forced their way through the crowd, seized the negro and made way with him.   A riot ensued, the arsenal was broken into, weapons secured, and the outraged populace, now fully armed, attacked the pursuers.

The authorities were powerless, and the mob took its own course till, finally, order was restored through the persuasive influence of one of the associate judges, and in the confusion the negro escaped.*

This high-handed procedure on the part of the slave-hunters and their utter contempt for the State Court aroused the deepest indignation throughout the State.   Many thought Ohio had disgraced herself by giving even a hearing to the Kentucky deputation for more efficient laws regarding the returning of runaway slaves.   Public sentiment became more pronounced in its views of slavery and returning fugitives.   There was an increasing disposition to throw upon the National government all responsibility for legislation respecting their capture.   This feeling culminated in 1843, when a strong influence was brought to bear upon the Legislature for the repeal of the Ohio Fugitive Slave Law, and a spirited discussion was had at the same time for the repeal of the "Black Laws."   The members were not yet ready for the repeal of both laws, but passed

* Niles' Register, 57:41.

a bill repealing the Fugitive Slave Law of 1839.*
From this time all slaves who escaped into Ohio
and were captured were tried and returned under the
exclusive authority of the United States laws, and
not that of the Ohio Fugitive Law.

Every year an increasing number of slaves found
their way through the Northern States, and the South
found more and more difficulty in securing their return.
The South was aroused to intense consternation, and
felt that a mighty effort must be made to secure
greater consideration for the return of their runaway
property. Just at this time, California applied for
admission to the Union, as a free State, which
afforded a favorable opportunity for the South to
make a "sharp bargain." The South agreed to its
admission as a free State and, in return, gained the
Fugitive Slave Law of 1850. "A law," said S. P.
Chase, " which authorizes and requires the appointment of two hundred and sixty commissioners and
an indefinite number of other officers to catch runaway slaves in the State of Ohio; which punishes
humanity as a crime; authorizes seizure without
process, trial without jury and consignment to slavery
beyond the limits of the State without the opportunity of defence and upon *ex parte* testimony."†
Such is the law which the Southern slave masters
forced upon the liberty-loving people of the North.
No wonder that Northern abhorrence and rebellion
found its expression in a greater sympathy for the
suffering slave, nor that the "business" of the
Underground Railroad was immensely stimulated.

A colored man, Elijah Anderson, who acted as

* January 19, 1843. Laws of Ohio, 41:13.
† Schucker's Life of Chase, p. 115.

general superintendent of the " road" leading into
Sandusky, claimed in 1855 to have conducted 1,000
slaves to freedom, and over eight hundred of this
number since 1850."*

The first case under the new law was against Mr.
Sloane of Sandusky, to whom reference has been
made several times, for the recovery of the value of
slaves whom it was claimed had escaped through his
connivance. The circumstances of the case were as
follows: In October, 1852, a party of fugitives
reached Sandusky, closely followed by their pursuers who, by act of the marshal, had been arrested
just as they were embarking for Canada. A
crowd quickly collected and the marshal had great
difficulty in taking his prisoners to the office of the
mayor, before whom they were to have their trial.
The office was filled with an excited crowd of blacks
and whites, eager to rescue the unfortunate fellows.
It is difficult to obtain an accurate account of what
took place in the office, as that given by one of the
principal actors, Mr. Sloane, differs essentially in
many points from that recorded in the court reports.† But it is not proposed here to enter at any
length upon the merits of the two sides; we simply
add that Mr. Sloane appeared in the office
in the capacity of a friend and defender of the
fugitives, and demanded by what warrant or other
legal papers they were held. Not receiving a satisfactory answer, he said he could see no authority for
holding the fugitives. At this the colored people

---

*Address of Rush R. Sloane referred to above.

†See Mr. Sloane's account in Magazine of Western History,
8:46-49. See also 6 McLean, p. 259 et seq.

"hustled them out" and they were never seen again in Sandusky.

The owner, through his agent, sued Sloane for the value of the slaves. The case was tried before the United States District Court, and the owner of three of the slaves secured judgment for $3,000.* For the remainder of them the verdict was given to Sloane, because the agent who caused their arrest did not have the power of attorney given him by their owners.† This case, with scores of similar cases, so increased the indignation of the people of Ohio against the iniquitous Fugitive Slave Law, that after seven years of endurance, Ohio, in common with other States, attempted to obstruct its execution by the passage of a "Personal Liberty Act." By this act it was made unlawful to confine in any jail, lock-up or guard-house in the State, any one charged simply with being a fugitive slave. The penalty for violating this act was imprisonment for not less than thirty nor more than ninety days, and a fine of any sum not exceeding $500.‡

This law is significant of the change in public sentiment within the State, but the real practical benefits were very few, and it was repealed in less than one year.§

Simultaneous with the passage of the Personal Liberty Act, the Legislature enacted more stringent legislation against kidnapping. The continual increase of fugitive slaves had developed a class of men who made it their business, without the slight-

---

†Weiner vs. Sloane, 6 McLean, p. 273.
*Gibbons vs. Sloane, 6 McLean, p. 259.
‡Passed April 16, 1857. Laws of Ohio, 54:170.
§Repealed February 28, 1858. Laws of Ohio, 55:10.

est scruple of conscience, to catch and return not only fugitives, but to seize free negroes and hustle them across the border and sell them in the Southern slave-markets. As early as 1819 the Legislature attempted to prohibit this practice, but the business was too profitable to be so easily checked.* In 1831 the law of 1819 was re-enacted and the penalty for its violation was imprisonment for not less than one year nor more than ten years.† In 1857 this law was amended, raising the minimum of imprisonment from one to three years and reducing the maximum to eight years.‡ This legislation reveals the growing sentiment against slavery.

Ohio was no longer to submit to the dictation of Southern slave-owners.

Two years later (1859) occurred one of the most famous cases in the entire history of Ohio in its relation to slavery. Our limits will permit only the briefest outline of the case. A whole volume has been written giving the details, but even this paper would be very incomplete with no reference to the Oberlin-Wellington Rescue case.§

The main facts are these: An Oberlin boy was promised twenty dollars by two Kentucky men if he would secure the person of a colored boy named John Rice. Under the pretence of furnishing him work, he led him into a secluded place, where were waiting for him the two Southern men. They at once seized him and hurried him off to Wellington,

---

*Passed January 25, 1819. Laws of Ohio, 55:10.
†Passed February 15, 1831. Laws of Ohio, 29:442.
‡Passed April 17, 1857. Laws of Ohio, 54:221.
§See History of the Oberlin-Wellington Rescue, by Jacob R. Shepherd.

a village about nine miles distant from Oberlin. They
were overtaken by a young college student, who
gave the alarm. The Cleveland *Leader* of April 14,
1895, gives an interesting account of his "taking
off" by one in whose home he was secreted till he
could be safely transported to Canada.*

The writer says: "The news was all over town
in a flash. Men left their business, their offices, and
rushed out to the streets, and took every vehicle they
found in the city, without a question. At Oberlin
College the classes did not wait to be dismissed. The
boys broke out from the college building bareheaded
and started to run to Wellington, joined in the race
by the professors. When the crowd reached the
hotel in Wellington, they found that John and the
men were still in the hotel. While they were dis-
cussing means of securing him, a big black man, who
was a freed man, dashed the door off its hinges where
John was held, picked John up on his shoulders and
rushed down the street, hastened him into a wagon, and
with breakneck speed drove him somewhere into the
country, no one knowing where. The two captors
did not dare to follow, and the citizens of Oberlin
having made good their boast that a slave should
never be taken from that town, quietly returned to
their homes." The writer very truthfully remarked:
"They were fast making anti-slavery sentiment
just then."

Thirty-seven citizens of Oberlin and Wellington
were indicted for violation of the law. For several
months the whole country was in a state of intense
excitement; complications grew more and more in-
tricate. The constitutionality of the Law of 1850

_____
*Mrs. J. M. Fitch's account in Cleveland *Leader*, April 14, 1895.

was questioned, and the State Supreme Court was called upon for a decision on that point. The court decided that as the United States Constitution, Art. iv., Sec. 2, provided for the return of fugitive slaves, citizens who should interfere in their capture were guilty of violation of law, whether the Law of 1793 or 1850 were Constitutional or not.*

The trial finally closed, by the slave-hunters themselves, who had been held for kidnapping, making a proposition to the effect that a mutual annulling of all indictment be made. The rescuers refused to be parties to such an agreement, but the United States authorities, nevertheless, accepted the proposition, and set the prisoners free. Thus ended the most memorable trial regarding the return of fugitive slaves on Ohio's records, and by it, not alone the freedom of the prisoners was gained, but freedom of public sentiment, whether expressed in private, in the court, or in the press.

The last escape made, according to Mr. Sloane, over the Sandusky division of the Underground Railroad, was that of two bright boys, who were hurried into Canada in the fall of 1861. It seems that a young Kentuckian remarked in a barroom that he was going to vote for Lincoln. His uncle, who was there, and the owner of twelve slaves, took a drink, and swore his young nephew should "ride a rail." The bartender, knowing the desperate character of the uncle, advised him to take his horse, which was already saddled, and make his escape. The young Lincoln champion made no loitering, but hastened with all speed to Maysville, dashed down the bank of the river and into a ferry boat, and made his

*Ohio State Reports, 9:77.

escape into Ohio, a free State, while his uncle and one-half dozen were in hot pursuit. He then vowed he would steal every one of his uncle's twelve slaves ; and true to his vow, he enticed them one by one till the two boys mentioned above were the last. The advent of the Civil War had now put an end to slavery, and there was therefore no longer any need for that hidden and mysterious work which had been so long in operation, and Mr. Levi Coffin, who had been considered as president of the Underground Railroad, resigned at a celebration of the adoption of the Fifteenth Amendment of the Constitution, held by the colored people in Cincinnati and vicinity. At the close of the exercises, as he was introduced by the chairman, he said, "I have held the position of president of the Underground Railroad for more than thirty years. The title was given to me by slave-hunters themselves who could not find their fugitive slaves after they got into my hands. I accepted the office thus conferred upon me and have endeavored to perform my duty faithfully. Government has now taken the work of providing for the slaves out of my hands. The stock of the Underground Railroad has gone down in the market, the business is spoiled ; it is of no farther use. I therefore resign my office and declare the operations of the Underground Railroad at an end."*

*Reminiscences of Levi Coffin, pp. 711, 712.

AUTHORITIES QUOTED.

American State Papers. Public Lands. Vol. 1. Miscellaneous, Vol. 1.

Atwater, Caleb, History of Ohio.

African Repository, Vol. 15, and August, 1831.

Burnett, Jacob, Notes on the Northwest Territory.

Benton, Thomas H., Thirty Years in the United States Senate.

Barber, A. D., Report on Condition of Colored People in Ohio, 1840.

Bancroft, George, History of the United States.

Barrett, J. A., Evolution of the Ordinance of 1787.

Birney, William, Life and Times of James G. Birney.

Coffin, Levi, Reminiscences of.

Cutler, W. P. and J. P., Life of Manasseh Cutler.

Cutler, J. P., Life of Ephraim Cutler.

Debates of Ohio Constitutional Convention, 1850-1.

Dunn, J. P., History of Indiana.

Fairchild, J. H., Oberlin; its Origin, Progress and results.

Fairchild, J. H., History of Oberlin Colony.

Garrison, William Lloyd, Life of, by His Children.

Hinsdale, B. A., The Old Northwest.

House (U. S.), Miscellaneous Documents 30th and 38th Congress.

Historical Magazine, July, 1869, Reprint of.

Minutes of the Ohio Constitutional Convention, 1803.

Hammond's Ohio Supreme Court Reports.

Kennedy, J. H., A Free Negro in the South. Magazine of Western History, 12 :130.

McLean's Reports (Law), Vol. 6.

Niles Register, Vols. 7, 11, 19, 21, 49, 57.

Ohio Reports (Law), Vols. 11, 12, 14, 19.

Ohio State Reports (Law), Vols. 6, 9.

Ohio House Journal, 1872–3.

Ohio Laws, Vols. 2, 5, 27, 29, 37, 41, 46, 51, 52, 53, 54, 55, 58, 64, 65, 66.

Ohio School Commissioner's Reports, 1853–1869.

Ohio State Executive Documents, 1863, Part 1.

Poole, W. P., Dr. Cutler and the Ordinance of 1787. North Amer. Rev., Vol. 122.

PAMPHLETS.

Proceedings of the Anti-Slavery Convention at Putnam, 1835.

Statement of Reasons Which Induced Students of Lane Seminary to Leave that Institution.

Reports of Ohio Anti-Slavery Society.

Autobiography of John Malvin.

Memorial of the Ohio Anti-Slavery Society to the General Assembly, 1838.

Minutes of Convention of Colored People, at Columbus, 1859.

Negro Suffrage and Equality, 1865.

Reid, Whitelaw, Ohio in the War.

Seward, W. H., Works of, Vol. 3.

Schucker's, J. W., Life of S. P. Chase.

Senate (U. S.), Journal, 16th Congress.

Senate (U. S.), Miscellaneous Documents, 34th Congress, Vol. 1.

Stanwood, Edward, History of Presidential Elections.

Sloane, Rush R., Underground Railroad in the Firelands—Firelands Pioneer (new series), Vol. 5. Magazine of Western History, Vol. 8.

Shipherd, Jacob R., History of the Oberlin–Wellington Rescue.

Siebert, William H., The Underground Railroad in Ohio; *The Archæologist*, February, 1895.

Warden, R. B., Life of S. P. Chase.

Wilson, Henry, Rise and Fall of the Slave Power in America.

Webster, Daniel, Works of, Vol. 3.

Williams, History of the Negro Race in America

Wright, Ohio Supreme Court Reports.

INDEX.

Years		1853.	1854.	1855.	1856.	1857.	1858.
Number of colored schools...		22	48	88	88	93	129
Number of scholars enrolled.		702	2,439	4,110	4,297	4,685	4,888
Number of teachers in colored schools					93	100	101	135
Average pay per month for teachers in white common schools	Males.		$28.00	25.02	26.70	27.71	27.89
	Females		$13.00	14.20	15.63	16.22	12.95
Average pay per month for teachers in colored schools	Males.		$21.75	25.40	25.73	27.28	27.24
	Females		$19.00	18.72	20.00	19.86	23.53
Number of colored youth between ages of 5 and 21.		6,862	9,756	10,516	10,500	11,582	12,562
Average length of session for white and col. schools.	White.		Months. 5 5-8 m.	6 1-10 m.	6 1-10 m.	5 m. 23 d.	6 m. 7 d. 6
	Colored.		4 5-7 m.	5 4-5 m.	5 4-5 m.	5 m. 11 d.	5 m. 2 d. 4
Number colored applicants for teachers' certificates.....								71

The above table is compiled from the Reports of the State Commissioner of Common Scho

60.	1861.	1862.	1863.	1864.	1865.	1866.	1867.	1868.	1869.	1886
159	168	172	167	145	143	157	182	189	204	....
512	6,902	7,456	7,229	....	7,409	7,509	10,086	10,404	10,075	11,27
151	174	174	164	....	164	163	219	241	238	221
.81	27.81	26.35	25.73	28.25	36.25	37.51	38.52	39.86	55.63	....
6.25	16.05	15.32	15.41	95	21.55	23.80	23.80	33.26	....	....
7.50	26.09	24.48	25.81	27.74	34.42	35.58	37.44	37.79	39.27	....
9.48	19.91	19.45	15.56	18.39	24.55	27.39	28.17	27.97	28.66	....
632	14,247	14,068	15,312	16,605	18,137	21,706	23,545	25,131	24,219	25,921
. 4 d.	6 m. 6 d.	6 m. 3 d.	....	25.15 w.	25.78 w.	27.29 w.	27.33 w.	27.81 w.	3.19 w.	31.
.7 d.	5 m. 8 d.	5 m. 6 d.	....	22.23 w.	26.66 w.	22.24 w.	21.56 w.	22.91 w.	24.96 w.	25.5 w
156	132	....	....	132	107	....	162	11	1	250

ears indicated.